100
MAGIC
TRICKS

100 MAGIC TRICKS

IAN ADAIR

CHARTWELL
BOOKS, INC.

To Maureen

A QUINTET BOOK

Published by Chartwell Books
A Division of Book Sales, Inc.
110 Enterprise Avenue
Secaucus, New Jersey 07094

This edition produced for sale in the U.S.A.,
its territories and dependencies only.

ISBN 1-55521-729-X

This book was designed and produced by
Quintet Publishing Limited
6 Blundell Street
London N7 9BH

Creative Director: Terry Jeavons
Designer: Chris Dymond
Project Editor: Judith Simons
Editor: Louise Bostock
Illustrator: Rob Shone
Photographer: Tim Cox

Typeset in Great Britain by
Central Southern Typesetters, Eastbourne
Manufactured in Hong Kong by
Regent Publishing Services Limited
Printed in Singapore by Star Standard Industries Pte. Ltd.

PUBLISHER'S NOTE

This book is not specifically aimed at children. If you do
buy this book for a child, please note that some of the tricks
involve the use of lighted matches, burning cigarettes and ignited
materials. In these cases, adult supervision is a necessity. Care
should *always* be taken to perform such effects in a
responsible manner.

CONTENTS

INTRODUCTION — WELCOME TO MAGIC

Welcome to the wonderful world of magic! Welcome to meeting magicians and sharing their magical secrets. And welcome to the pages of this book, which I hope will put you on the road to success, whether magic or conjuring be an enjoyable hobby or your destined profession.

Magic or conjuring offers bewilderment, colour, excitement and mystery. But it must always *entertain* those who are involved, either as spectators or participants. Perfecting magical techniques and putting them into practice is one thing, but it is quite another to actually go out and face an audience, knowing that they are waiting to be entertained. Pure bewilderment is not enough, and the student of magic will soon realize that clever patter, rehearsed movements and keeping control of numbers are as important as the secrets of the tricks he or she has to execute.

This book shows that in magic, there are many fascinating avenues to explore. There are magic dealers who specialize in selling professional properties; there are magic conventions, dinners and events, social functions attended by all the stars of magic. Magic conventions offer seminars, lectures and demonstrations and teach-ins, many of which are invaluable to the novice. There are magic clubs and societies, large and small, all over the world. The reader of this book will also soon realize that there are many branches of magic, and that each branch suits particular personalities. This book covers several of the major branches of magic, giving details of important techniques and a host of individual tricks to perfect. It also gives advice on presentation before an audience, large or small.

Buying a book of magic does not automatically make you a magician, but with practice and interest, you could go a long way.

★ THE RULES OF MAGIC ★

Every game, profession or organization has certain rules to adhere to; some we accept, some we like and others we dislike intensely.

The first, and perhaps only, rule of magic, is that a magician never gives away the secrets of magic. Magicians performing tricks never reveal the secrets after their performance. The audience's enjoyment of magic is to a certain extent due to the mystery of how the magic happened. To tell the secret of a trick is to deny the audience this enjoyment. The audience feel that although they were at first entertained, they have now been cheated, and quite rightly so. The first rule of magic is to keep the secret.

Can you keep a secret?

★ PRACTICE ★

Practice is the learning of individual effects and routines, and the rehearsal of a complete act from start to finish. Theatrical people use the word rehearsal as a run-through with a cast or partner, and a dress rehearsal is just as it should be on the night.

Professionals and amateurs alike joke that it will be all right on the night – but will it? The wise and discerning performer understands that only practice and attention to detail make for trouble-free performances. To achieve this, one must have patience, time and understanding.

I remember seeing a very enthusiastic student of magic rush into a performance without planning his programme. He fumbled, dropped items, forgot his patter lines and generally made a fool of himself. His appearance was good, his tricks and execution fair, but his presentation left much to be desired. He had forgotten to practice his movements, as well as his tricks. While it is admirable to perform a trick cleverly, it is unwise to disregard the way in which move-

ments should be executed. There is nothing worse than seeing a clumsy magician, in the middle of his act, bending down to retrieve his apparatus, and setting it out again in front of his audience.

Practising in front of a mirror is good training, but not always the best. When working to a mirror, there is a tendency to stand in the same position, which means that a public performance could well appear static. I know of one young man who used his bedroom in which to practise his act. In front of the mirror, one by one, he discarded each trick – on the nearby bed. When he presented his act on stage before a live audience, there was no mirror, and there was certainly no bed. The performer had not worked out where he would discard all his unwanted apparatus. It was not all right on the night – his act was a flop.

Practise walking on and off, never turning your back to the audience, unless of course the effect or routine demands it. Taking a bow may seem easy, but can often look a

farce when executed by someone who feels silly. When the trick has come to its climax, the performer needs to clearly signal this to the audience – a smile, arms opening upwards and a slight bow achieves the right effect for the wise performer who wants to go home that evening well and truly satisfied with his performance.

The wise student should practise each trick so much that he or she could almost perform them blindfolded. If the student aims to come over professionally, he or she must practise again and again, until every little detail is embedded in the mind. Slow, smooth and elegant hand gestures should also be practised. The magician should appear graceful and compelling, and should know how to handle spectators.

One top television magician told me that he has now practised his act so much that, while he appears in front of a live audience or before the cameras, he is thinking about what he is going to eat after the show! Now that's show business.

SELECTING THE ★ CORRECT BRANCH OF MAGIC ★

Some magicians present a mixed bag of tricks and illusions drawn from many different branches of magic, others specialize in one form – mentalism, say, or close-up magic. In making a choice of which field to enter, one must be careful. So often, enthusiastic beginners choose the wrong branches of magic to present, ending in disaster.

If you happen to like comedy magic – that is ordinary magic laced with comedy patter – then stick to it. Think again if you are someone

who does not excite people very much and cannot tell funny jokes or stories. It could be that you will never be able to become a comedy magical entertainer.

If, on the other hand, you feel that your approach is better at reaching more mature audiences, a serving of mentalism may be the answer. If so, be sure you can deliver direct and dramatic lines. Make sure your face fits the picture. Do you look like a person who reads minds and predicts the future?

If you simply wish to be a jack of all trades, and want to entertain your friends, you cannot be categorized in any way – you are just a general magician. Relax, look at the tricks in this book, learn them and select the ones you like best. Practise each trick and master the various methods of presentation, then use the ones you are more confident at performing and go out to entertain your public. Select the times when you wish to perform and never perform under pressure.

★ THE ORIGINS OF MAGIC ★

LEFT Robert Houdin (1805–71), the French conjurer and magician, was celebrated for his optical illusions and became known as the Father of Modern Magic. Houdin was the first to use electromagnetism for his effects.

RIGHT *Jongleurs* (jugglers) first appeared in Europe during the Middle Ages; they journeyed from town to village entertaining their audiences with juggling and acrobatics, sword-swallowing and fire-eating. The tradition of the street entertainer persists to this very day.

RIGHT Harry Houdini (1874–1926), born Erich Weiss, adopted his stage name from Robert Houdin, whose memoirs he read as a young boy. He was practised in many fields of magic but became world famous as an escapologist.

Magic in human culture is as old as the hills. Records show that as far back as 50,000 BC, magic was being practised by cave-dwellers, probably as part of their religious rituals. The first written evidence of a magician appears in ancient Egyptian texts dating to *c* 2000 BC. These writings, known as the Westcar Papyrus, describe a performance by Dedi of Dedsnefu, in which he cut off the head of a duck and a pelican, and restored each without harming either animal.

In the Middle Ages, it seems that most people believed in magic, which was still closely connected with religion in that Christian teaching considered magic practices sinful, and persecuted practitioners as such. Magic was also involved in the healing of the sick. Up until the 1700s, many people who practised magic were burned as witches.

The first Europeans who made their living by performing magic tricks as entertainment made their appearance during

the Middle Ages. They were known by the French name *jong-leurs* (jugglers), and were strolling players who swallowed swords, ate fire, sang and danced, and probably performed the famous cups and balls trick for anyone who would wager against them.

Gradually, the modern magician's repertoire grew as performers made appearances in local fairs and, for the first time in the 19th century, in the music halls.

Today, there is a long list of magicians whom we remember as phenomenal performers, including John Henry Anderson (billed as The Great Wizard of the North), David Devant, Robert Houdin (the Father of Modern Magic), Horace Goldin, Harry Houdini, Chung Ling Soo, Ching Ling Foo, The Great Lafayette, Harry Bouton, The Great Dante, Paul Daniels, and David Copperfield. Each has added his own mark to the history of magic performance with new concepts and routines, new forms of presentation and angles, making it the varied and fascinating world we find today.

THE KING OF HANDCUFFS

MAGIC DEALERS –
THEIR ROLE IN SERVING
★ THE MAGICIAN ★

The magic dealer is a maker of magic; he makes magic in various materials, markets his products, and then sells his wares through various channels. Most dealers offer a mail-order service, which they advertise in magazines; some larger concerns issue their own catalogues or magazines in which they advertise their range of theatrical properties.

Having been associated with magic dealing for over three decades, I find that magic dealers can be listed in three categories. First is the magic shop, often a joke shop, selling whoopee cushions, novelties and toys. Only one small section of the shop may be devoted to magic, or to the sale of professional conjuring props. The selection of items is usually very basic. Although some professional material is available, only classic effects are ordered by the proprietor who, incidentally, very rarely knows anything about the art of magic.

Second is the small mail-order firm, which usually advertises in magic magazines. Many do not have proper premises, and it is often hard to find those who do. Most magic dealers work from one room of their house, say a spare room which they have turned into a stockroom. Mail-order dealers send goods through the post, and some provide a fast and efficient service, even if they only advertise a small number of products within their range.

Third is the more professional magic dealer who works on a much larger scale. Such dealers have a good knowledge of what customers require and a wide range of products, classic and modern. Some publish their own magic magazine which furthers sales of their products. The professional magic dealer never relies upon the sales of jokes and novelties to enhance his sales of professional theatrical equipment.

JOINING MAGIC CLUBS
★ AND SOCIETIES ★

Magic is no different from any other hobby or profession in that there are many clubs, societies and organizations to join. The famous Magic Circle, formed in 1905, started with just a few magicians and, over a period of years, it has attracted more and more members so that there are now some 1,800 members across the world.

Membership of the Magic Circle depends on merit, and there is a strict hierarchy of membership. Associate members progress to full membership, eventually becoming associate and then full members of the Inner Magic Circle. The Magic Circle has its own meeting place in London, and magicians meet regularly to share ideas, discuss new tricks and hear visiting speakers.

A similar organization is the International Brotherhood of Magicians, with headquarters in the United States. Although larger than the Magic Circle, the International Brotherhood of Magicians has no regular meeting place. Members keep in touch with each other through the pages of the official magazine, *The Budget*, a monthly publication distributed only to members. The major event of the year is the Annual Convention, often attracting two thousand or more magicians. Lectures, dealers' demonstrations, gala shows, teach-ins, close-up sessions and many other interesting aspects of magic are planned each year to keep magicians informed and on their toes.

The majority of the smaller magic societies draw perhaps only 20 or 30 members from the local area, but they are all dedicated to learning and practising the art of magic.

Annual subscription fees differ from one club to the other; it is often the case that members of a small society are members of both the Magic Circle in London and the International Brotherhood of Magicians. Some magicians become members of several organizations connected with magic, so as to enjoy a well-balanced and varied outlook on what is happening in the world of magic.

Joining a magic club or society can be a most enjoyable experience, one shared by all members who participate, each endeavouring to elevate the craft to the highest standard possible.

SUBSCRIBING TO
★ MAGIC MAGAZINES ★

Most beginners do not realize that there are such things as magic magazines, produced especially for the student of magic, perhaps because they are not available from the newsagents. Such insiders periodicals are available on subscription only.

There are some 22 periodicals internationally available at the moment. Some appear quarterly and some monthly, but there is only one weekly magazine of magic – *Abracadabra*. Goodliffe the Magician, well known in his day, and still a name to conjure with, first published this magazine some 44 years ago. Today, Donald Bevan, who has been responsible for 30 years of continued production, has managed to release the magazine weekly without fail. Monthly magazines include *The Magigram*, a 72-page magazine of magic which is distributed worldwide; it covers 80 different countries, including the Soviet Union, and is printed on the premises of The Supreme Magic Company in the UK. The same company also produces a sister magazine *The Trixigram*, a publication which brings the magician news, views and reviews on the magic scene. A recent magazine of magic, *Alakazam*, is aimed at children's entertainers.

★ ADVERTISING AND PUBLICITY ★

The subject of promoting oneself as a performer arises once the student of magic has brought together a complete series of tricks, practised them until he or she is perfect, and has established a show ready for presentation to the public. There are many ways in which to promote and advertise. The most obvious place to start is the classified telephone directory or local newspaper. The advantages of these publications are relatively cheap advertising, in a restricted locale.

However you advertise, whether it be in magazines or newspapers, or even in the window of a local shop, your advertisement must be literate, informative, and well laid out. Poor copy material never results in bookings, and an over-elaborate ad confuses the public.

A very good method of obtaining superb publicity – for free– is to supply a story of news interest to the local or national press. Not only does a news story act as free advertising, it also takes up more space than the average ad, giving you even more exposure. Here is an example . . . One magician I know advertised every week, but without much success. One week he concocted a story that his magic rabbit had vanished from its hutch, and this received not only local but national coverage. He obtained more show bookings from that article alone than from all his paid advertisements.

Photographs, pictures, business cards, leaflets and flyers, and give-away trivia all help to promote you and your show. Balloons printed with your name, magic posters for the children to colour, magic 'money' to give away amuses and excites, and pictures of the rabbit which assisted you in the show simply makes them all want to take the printed card home.

Promoting your show can be as much fun as practising the tricks and presenting the act, yet in considering promotion one must always be aware that *you* are the commodity being promoted. In doing so, you must try to emphasize your better features and talents, but always tell the truth.

SIMPLE SLEIGHT OF HAND AND MANIPULATION

All accomplished magicians make sure that they have mastered sleight of hand. It is important for several reasons. First, your movements will appear more polished, even when using other props. Second, if such props let you down, you can always rely upon sleight of hand to get through. Third, your routines will be more varied and entertaining if sleight of hand sequences are introduced in between other effects.

A great deal of time and patience must be devoted to perfecting the techniques but, once mastered, your skills will be a source of great amusement to all. It is important to ensure that finger nails are cut and clean, and that sleeve cuffs are presentable.

★ CARDS ★

PALMING CARDS

Many of the card effects performed by magicians and manipulators are achieved by palming cards. Here are two classic card palms.

Flat-palm version

ABOVE Place the card flat in the palm of the hand and hold the card facing towards you. From the audience's viewpoint (see inset), the card cannot be seen and the hand position looks natural.

Curled-in version

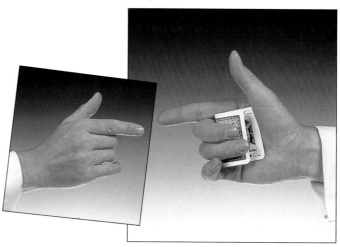

ABOVE With the card held flat in the palm, curl the fingers in, bending the card over. Invisible to the audience, this version allows you to adopt a different hand position (see inset).

PRODUCING CARDS
· · · · ☆ ☆ ☆ · · · ·

Producing single cards from the hand

First a card is seen between the fingers, next it is made to vanish and then reappear again.

1 Display the card to the audience.

2 Grip the sides of the card with the first and little fingers, bend the middle fingers down behind the card and use the thumb to pivot the card over . . .

3 . . . like this. Using the middle fingers to control the card, continue the move so that the card disappears from view to be held . . .

4 . . . in the back-palm position.

5 Hold the hand side-on to the audience and reverse the pivot.

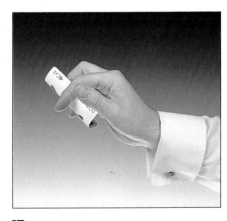

6 Use the fingers to draw the card into the palm position.

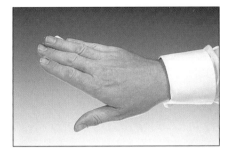

7 Hold the back of the hand towards the audience to show that the card has once again disappeared from view.

8 Repeat Steps 1 – 3 to bring the card to the back-palm position again.

9 To produce the card, reach up into the air and at the same time pivot the card up into the hand.

Producing several cards from the hand

The same pivoting action is used to produce a succession of cards from a stack held secretly in the hand. Again, the effect is of cards being plucked from the air.

1 Hold the stack in the back-palm position and pivot the stack into the hand . . .

2 . . . like this.

3 Peel off the first card from the stack with the thumb and pivot the stack to the back-palm position . . .

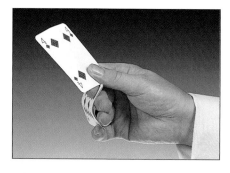

4 . . . like this.

5 Repeat the sequence, discarding the first card and producing a second and so on until the stack is exhausted.

Producing cards – a variation

Most magicians produce cards with the palm of the right or left hand facing the audience, plucking cards out of the air. In this variation the cards are produced while the left hand is clenched towards the audience.

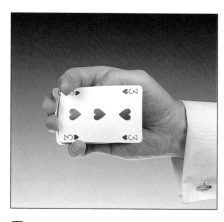

1 Conceal a stack of cards within the palm.

2 Grip the pack with the fingers. Peel off the first card with the thumb . . .

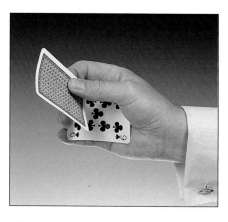

3 . . . and produce it to the audience between the thumb and first finger.

4 The audience's view of the produced card. Repeat the sequence to produce more cards, discarding each in turn.

★ VANISHING HALF A PACK ★

During card-manipulation routines, a neat vanish of half a pack is visually effective.

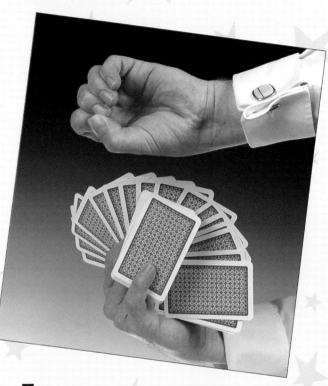

3 The back view showing the half pack held in the right hand behind the fan.

1 Display half a pack of cards, squared-up, in the left hand and fan the remainder of the pack in the right hand.

2 Obscure the left hand with the fan of cards, and secretly grip the half pack with the free fingers of the right hand. At the same time turn the left hand and form it into a fist.

4 From the front view again, open the left fist to show that the half pack has vanished and gather the entire pack together in the right hand.

Producing fans of cards

The back-palm position again plays a major part in producing fans of cards. The effect is that the magician produces a fan and drops it into a receptacle and then magically produces further fans from thin air, discarding each. In fact, each fan produced is split, with the majority of the cards being pivoted to the back-palm position ready to produce the next fans, while just a few of the top cards are discarded.

3 . . . like this.

4 The start of the pivoting move seen from the back view.

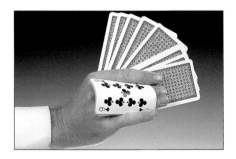

5 The completion of the pivot, again from the back view, with the stack in back-palm position.

1 Fan the stack of cards towards the audience.

2 Curl the third and little fingers round the bottom of the fan to pivot the majority of the stack to the back-palm position . . .

6 Discard the remaining few cards in the fan, then pivot the stack back into the hand to produce the next fan.

★ THIMBLES ★

PRODUCING THIMBLES
· · · · ☆ ☆ ☆ · · · ·

Producing a single thimble

A thimble is apparently plucked from the air to appear on the magician's thumb.

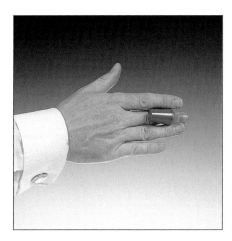

1 Secretly hold the thimble at the back of the hand in the finger-palm position, gripped between the first and third fingers, and present the hand palm-on to the audience.

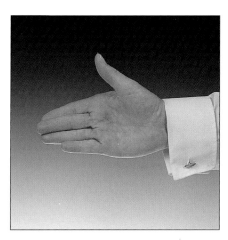

2 To the audience, the thimble is invisible.

3 Pivot the thimble into the hand and . . .

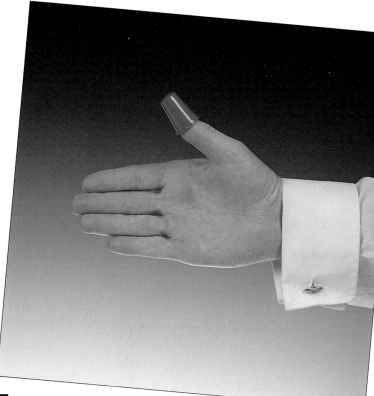

4 . . . onto the thumb as you apparently pluck the thimble from the air.

★ SHOWING THE HANDS EMPTY ★

This technique is also applied to the thumb-tip (see chapter 3, Classics of Conjuring).

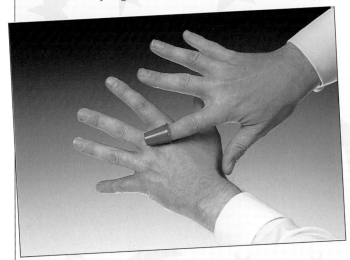

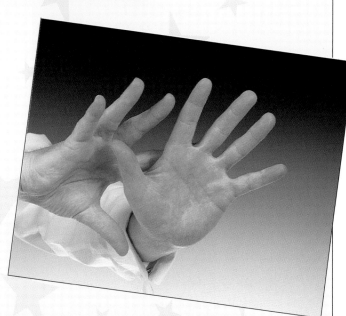

1 Conceal the first finger, wearing the thimble, behind the back of the opposite hand.

2 To the audience, the hands appear empty.

Producing a succession of thimbles

The thumb-crutch position, or thumb palm, is used to conceal a stack of thimbles.

ABOVE Grip a stack of thimbles in the fleshy part of the hand between thumb and first finger in the thumb-crutch position. To produce a succession of thimbles, one after the other, simply pivot a finger down onto the thimble on top of the stack, and repeat, passing the thimbles from one hand to another.

★ A THIMBLE HOLDER ★

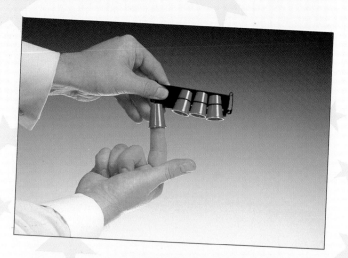

ABOVE The thimble holder is an aid which allows the performer to secretly and easily acquire one or more thimbles while leaving the hands free. The thimbles slide easily from the thimble holder; it is usually attached and concealed inside the jacket.

VANISHING THIMBLES
· · · · ☆ ☆ ☆ · · · ·

Poke-in thimble vanish

To make a thimble vanish in a convincing manner, this method is hard to beat.

1 Display the thimble on the first finger of the right hand and poke this finger into the left hand.

2 Seen from the rear view, as you close the left hand to form a fist, curl the thimble finger inwards, bringing the thimble into the thumb-crutch position.

3 To the audience, the left hand appears to be holding the first finger *and* the thimble.

4 Remove the first finger of the right hand and point towards the closed left fist to reinforce the suggestion that the thimble has been retained in the left hand.

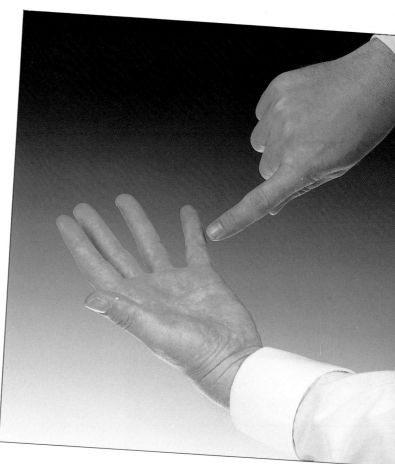

5 Open the left fist to complete the vanish. The thimble is still concealed in the right hand.

A simple thimble vanish

A thimble is thrown up into the air and magically vanishes.

1 Display the thimble on the first finger.

2 Make an upward throwing motion with the hand and at the same time curl the first finger towards the crutch of the thumb.

3 Seen from the rear view, immediately release the thimble and hold it in the thumb-crutch position.

4 To the audience, the hand, having completed the throw, appears empty.

★ BALLS ★

PALMING A BALL

· · · · ☆ ☆ ☆ · · · ·

Palm grip

A ball will adhere to the palm of the hand, if the hand is moist or has been smeared with a moisturizing cream.

ABOVE Seen from the rear, the ball clings to the palm. Keep the hand in a natural position, ensuring the ball is invisible to the audience.

Finger-grip palm

This variation allows the performer to adopt a different hand position.

ABOVE Seen from the rear, grip the ball between the palm and lower three fingers.

ABOVE To the audience, the hand position, with the index finger pointing, looks natural, and the ball is completely concealed.

VANISHING A BALL

· · · · ☆ ☆ ☆ · · ·

Here are three different vanishes to practise and master.

Take-away vanish

1 Rest the ball on top of the clenched right fist, and bring the left hand, held in a cupped fashion, towards the right as if to take the ball.

2 Pretend to take the ball away from the right fist and at the same time . . .

3 . . . drop the ball into the right fist (seen from the rear).

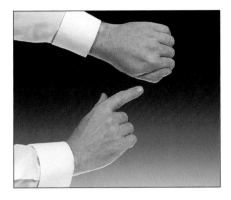

4 From the front again, with the ball in the finger-grip palm position, point to the left fist and . . .

5 . . . slowly open the fingers of the left hand to show the vanish.

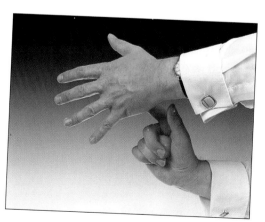

6 The rear view shows the ball concealed in the right hand.

Poke-in vanish

1 Clench the left hand around ball, holding the fist side on to the audience so the ball is visible, and bring the right hand up underneath the left.

2 Poke the ball into the fist with the right thumb, allowing the right hand to cup underneath the left.

3 At the same time allow the ball to drop into the right hand (seen from the rear).

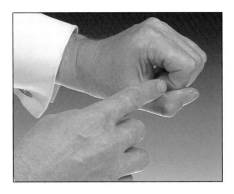

4 With the ball held in the finger-grip palm position, poke the 'ball' into the left fist again with the index finger, to reinforce the belief that the ball is still in the left hand.

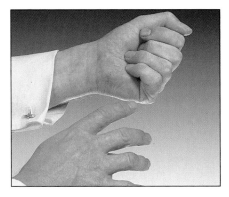

5 Turn the left hand over, and with the ball now held in the palm-grip position in the right hand . . .

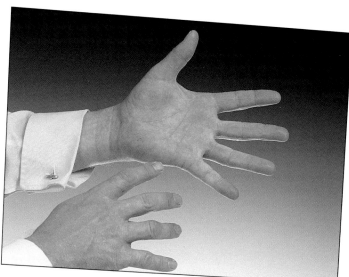

6 . . . slowly open the fingers of the left hand to reveal the vanish.

Lift-up vanish

3 With the ball in the finger-grip palm position, point to the clenched left fist and . . .

1 Hold the ball in the palm of the right hand and move the left hand towards it as if to take away the ball.

4 . . . slowly open the fingers of the left hand to reveal the vanish.

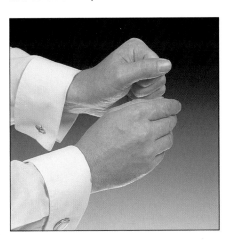

2 As the left hand supposedly grips away the ball, turn the right hand over so that the back of the hand points towards the audience, and retain the ball in this hand.

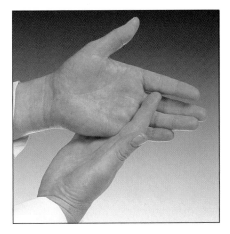

5 For a further effect, partially turn the right hand to face the audience, pivoting the ball behind the back of the open left hand.

★ CIGARETTES ★

PRODUCING CIGARETTES

· · · · · ☆ ☆ ☆ · · · ·

Producing a single cigarette

A cigarette can be secretly palmed and produced as if from thin air using the following method.

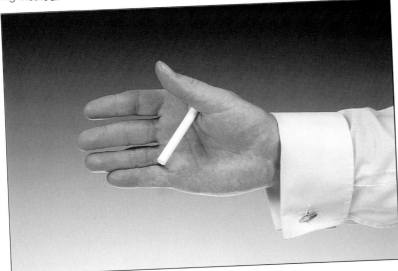

1 Grip the cigarette in the thumb-crutch position. From the front the hand will appear natural and the cigarette will be completely concealed.

2 For the production, curl the fingers inwards to grip the cigarette.

3 Then, in one swift and elegant move, display the cigarette between the first and second fingers.

Repeat production

The same technique described above can be applied here.

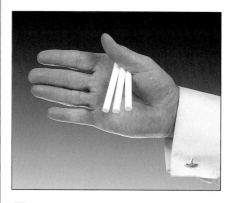

1 Secretly conceal a stack of cigarettes – as many as you can hold – in the thumb-crutch position.

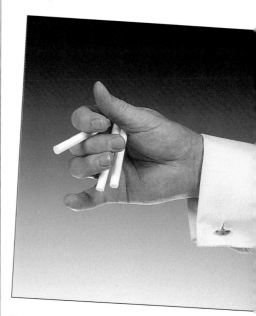

2 Curl the fingers inwards and grip the first cigarette between the first and second fingers. Repeat the action to produce the entire stack, one by one.

Hat production

In effect, the magician displays a folded opera hat, opens it and then produces, one by one, a whole stream of cigarettes, which he discards, one by one, into the hat. He then empties the hat onto a table. In fact, the magician produces only *one* cigarette.

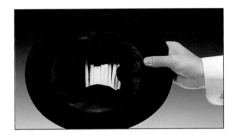

1 For the set-up, use an opera-hat and insert the cigarettes between the springs.

2 In performance, display the top of the hat to the audience. Because the hat is folded flat the audience will be convinced that it is empty. With a simple striking motion, open the hat, secretly releasing the cigarettes into the bottom.

3 Produce a cigarette from the air and as you appear to discard it into the hat, pivot the cigarette into the thumb-crutch position. Repeat the action, producing the same cigarette, until the required number have been 'produced' and 'discarded'.

★ RISING CIGARETTE ★

In between the productions and vanishes of cigarettes, it is nice to introduce a flourish or two. This particular flourish looks good and blends in with most cigarette sequences. In effect, a cigarette clenched within the fist mysteriously rises out of the hand.

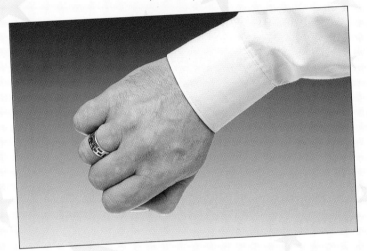

1 Hold the cigarette within the hand, with the thumb tucked inside, resting on the base of the cigarette. Face the back of the hand towards the audience.

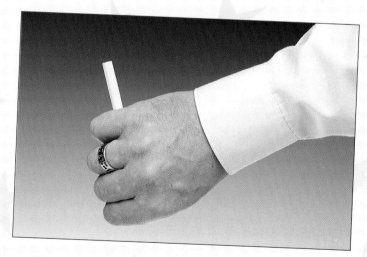

2 Push the cigarette up with the thumb so that it slowly rises from the clenched fist.

STEALING CIGARETTES FROM
★ A BOX OF MATCHES ★

This technique allows the performer to keep his hands free prior to producing from a stack of cigarettes. The cigarettes are placed in a matchbox – one end of the inner tray is cut away – and the matchbox is kept at the back of the working area, hidden by other pieces of apparatus.

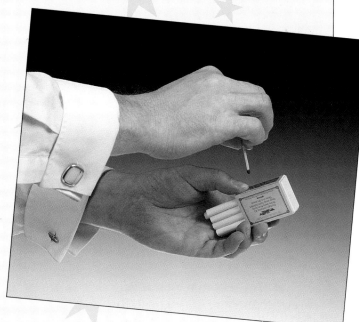

ABOVE Pick up the matchbox and hold it so that the cut-away end and the protruding cigarettes point into the hand. To the audience, the cigarettes are concealed, the box looks genuine and the hand position appears natural, especially when holding the box to strike a match.

ABOVE Seen from the rear, tilt the box slightly so that the cigarettes slide out to be concealed in the hand ready for production.

VANISHING CIGARETTES
· · · · ☆ ☆ ☆ · · · ·

Poke-in vanish

This is accomplished in exactly the same manner as described in the previous section on balls (see page 22). The effect is that a cigarette is poked into the performer's left fist with the right thumb, only for the left hand to open to show that the cigarette has vanished. The right hand then plucks the vanished cigarette out of the air. In fact, the cigarette is secretly dropped into the right hand and concealed there until the production is made.

Take-away vanish

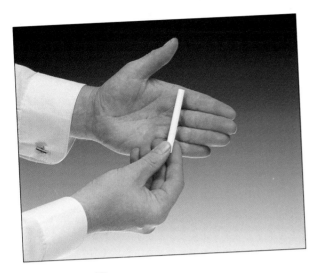

1 Display the cigarette between the first finger and thumb of the right hand.

2 Cup the left hand over the cigarette as if to take it, and at the same time pivot the cigarette into the right hand.

3 Form a fist with the left hand and secretly bring the cigarette into the thumb-crutch position in the right hand.

4 Rub the back of the clenched fist. The right hand appears to be empty.

5 Open the fingers of the left hand to complete the vanish.

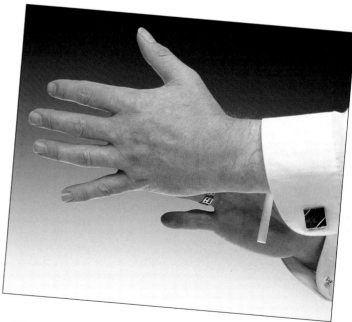

6 Seen from the rear, the cigarette can be seen firmly held in the thumb-crutch position.

★ COINS ★

PRODUCING AND VANISHING ★ A COIN ★

To produce a single coin out of the air, or indeed from someone's clothing, this method is simple and effective when put into action. Incidentally, the same coin can be vanished by reversing the procedure.

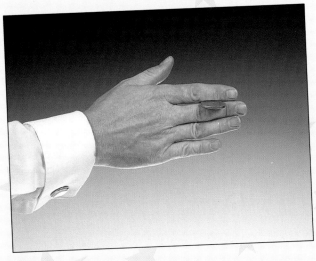

1 Secretly hold the coin at the back of the hand, gripped between the first and second fingers.

3 To produce the coin, pivot the fingers inwards and . . .

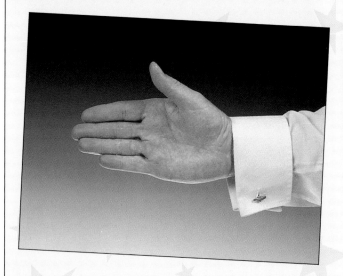

2 Show the hand palm-on so that the audience sees that it is apparently empty.

4 . . . use the thumb to bring the coin out from the back position so it appears for all to see.

★ PRODUCING SEVERAL COINS ★

1 Conceal a stack of coins within the crutch of the thumb.

2 Hold the hand palm-on so that the audience sees that the hand is apparently empty.

3 Curl the thumb upwards and peel off the top coin from the stack. Repeat the procedure until all the coins are produced.

CLEVER CARD TRICKS

It is not unusual for the beginner in magic to start with card tricks. I did when I was a boy magician and so did many of my magician friends. A pack of cards is inexpensive, and usually available at home anyway, which means that the budding magician is involved in little or no expense. Do not forget, however, that practice makes perfect.

Card tricks can be presented almost any-where – on a table, on the floor or even in the hands of the performer. Some magicians use a close-up mat to work on, the spread of cards showing up well against the flock-covered surface of a contrasting colour. Others prefer to use a bar counter or table.

As for the cards themselves, some magicians prefer cards which have a linen finish, others prefer the surfaces to be plastic-coated. Avoid using cheap, badly made cards. These tend to crack when even slightly bent and do not wear well. If using your own pack of cards, powder them on both sides with zinc stereate to make the complete pack easy to handle and perfect to fan. In selecting a pack for yourself, try and obtain one which has a common back design, of the type audiences are familiar with. Bent, torn and defaced cards never assist the performer, because audiences will automatically think these are blatant markings for the benefit of the performer.

UPON REFLECTION

This amazing card trick can be repeated several times without spectators detecting its secret.

Effect

A spectator is requested to select a card from a pack by pushing the blade of a table knife into it and noting the card above the blade. Needless to say, the performer correctly reveals the name of the chosen card.

Apparatus

A regular pack of cards and a table knife that has a shiny blade.

Working and Presentation

Ask a member of the audience to shuffle the pack of cards and then to hold the pack in his left hand, cards facing downwards. Hand the table knife to the spectator and ask him to select a card by pushing the blade in between any section of cards. Finally, ask the spectator to note the selected card above the knife blade.

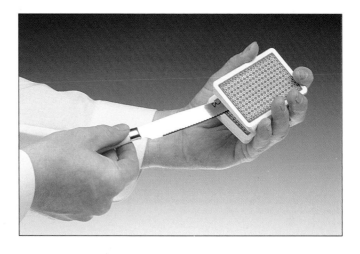

LEFT The selected card's suit and value is clearly reflected in the shiny knife blade.

Take the pack from the spectator and with the knife still lodged between the cards, lift the top portion so that you can secretly glimpse a reverse reflection of the suit and value of the selected card. The polished blade makes this possible and you need only lift the portion of cards slightly. However, it is important to position the knife blade towards the bottom left corner where the card's suit and value appears.

You can now reveal the name of the chosen card. Declare the colour of the suit first, then the value of the card, to make the presentation more impressive.

MYSTIC FIVE

· · · · ☆ ☆ ☆ · · · ·

All you require for this trick is a pack of ordinary playing cards.

Effect

A card is freely selected from the pack by a member of the audience. It is replaced in top position, and the pack is cut. The magician explains that one card will magically reverse itself in the pack, and its value will denote the position of the chosen card. When the pack is fanned, a card – for example, the five of hearts – is seen to be reversed, and believe it or not, the fifth card to follow it is the chosen one.

Apparatus

A pack of cards.

Set-up

Before the start of the presentation, remove a five-spot card, reverse it and replace it in the pack, so that it becomes the fifth card from the bottom of the pack.

Working and Presentation

Fan the pack making sure the audience is not aware of the reversed card. Request a spectator to select a card and then to return it to the top of the pack.

Make a complete cut of the pack bringing the reversed card towards the centre of the pack. Fan the pack to show the reversed card. State that the value of the reversed card will denote the exact position of the card selected by the spectator. Count along five cards and the fifth card will automatically be the chosen one.

Five-spot card

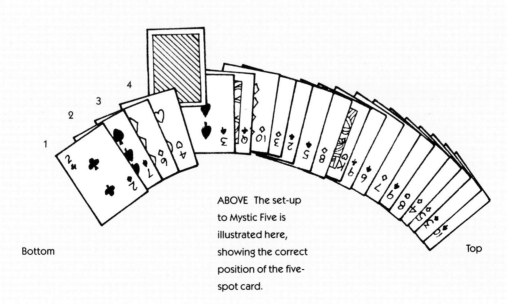

ABOVE The set-up to Mystic Five is illustrated here, showing the correct position of the five-spot card.

Bottom

Top

RED AND BLACK SEPARATION

• • • • ☆ ☆ ☆ • • • •

Here, the performer appears to accomplish the impossible, a miracle which can be presented with a normal pack of cards, even a borrowed one.

Effect

A pack of cards is shown to the audience and shuffled. All 52 cards are spread facedown on a table. Skilfully, the performer divines the colour of each card, red or black.

Apparatus

A regular pack of cards.

Set-up

Before or during your magical performance, secretly arrange the pack so that the red pip cards are separated from the black ones.

With both blocks of cards separate, secretly bend both, reds up and blacks down.

Working and Presentation

You will find that even when the cards are shuffled together and then spread facedown on the table, it is quite easy for you to see which are the red cards and which are the black. In divining the colour of each card, simply point here and there, touching each card and revealing their colours.

Afterwards, secretly remove the curves by just flexing the pack.

ABOVE To set up this trick, separate the red pip cards from the black ones, and bend the red block upwards and the black downwards, as shown.

TRIPLE CARD DIVINATION

· · · · ☆ ☆ ☆ · · · ·

The performer will receive credit for being a clever diviner of cards
in this trick, one which can be performed in close-up and
surrounded by the audience.

Effect

A pack of cards is shuffled by a member of the audience and returned to the performer, who spreads them face-down on the table. Touching one face-down card, the performer states its suit and value – the card is placed to one side. Two other cards from the spread are pointed to by the performer, and their names are declared aloud. When all three cards are reversed they are found to be the ones that the magician divined.

Apparatus

A regular pack of cards.

Working and Presentation

Ask a member of the audience to shuffle the pack. Take the pack from the spectator and secretly glimpse at the bottom card of the pack and remember it. (For our purpose, the bottom card is the six of spades.) Spread the cards over the surface of the table, face-down. Although the cards may be spread haphazardly, you must be able to locate the card which was at the bottom of the pack.

In divining the first of the three cards, touch the back of any card stating it is a black card, a six – the six of spades – announcing the name of the bottom card. Remove the first card from the spread, but secretly note its value before placing it to the side. Touch a second card and announce the name of the first card just noted. Remove this second card, too, and place it to the side near the first one, again noting its value.

To divine the third card, touch the card which was originally at the bottom of the pack and announce the name of the second card just noted. Place this card with the other two.

Pick up and reverse all three cards to show that they are indeed the cards that you have just named.

LEFT How can you correctly divine the suit and value of three cards from a shuffled pack spread out, face-down, on a table? See above for the answer.

ELIMINATION

· · · · ☆ ☆ ☆ · · · ·

Magicians have been using elimination methods for many years. In the following trick, elimination is used to restrict a spectator's supposedly free choice.

Effect

The performer holds up a playing card to reveal only its back design. The card is placed inside an envelope, which is sealed and handed to a spectator.

A series of questions is directed towards the spectator, a quick answer each time coming back to the performer, until the name of a playing card is decided by the spectator himself. Needless to say, the card named by the spectator is the card that was placed inside the envelope.

Apparatus

An envelope and a playing card of any suit and value. The three of diamonds has been selected for the following example.

Working and Presentation

Display the back of the playing card to the audience and seal it inside the envelope. Then hand the envelope to a spectator to take charge of during the experiment. Obtain the services of a second spectator and begin a series of questions. 'Think of one of the colours – red or black?' The spectator answers red. If that is the colour of the card, and it is in our case, well and good, but if the spectator says black, reply, 'That leaves us with red'. Ask the second question. 'A picture or a plain card?' The spectator answers plain, and all is well. Once again, if the spectator answers picture, say, 'That leaves us with plain'.

Continue, 'Red was chosen, please mention one of the two suits, hearts or diamonds. If the spectator chooses diamonds say, 'Fine'; if he answers hearts, again use the elimination process saying 'That leaves us with diamonds'. Ask further 'Now, do you want high or low numbers?' If low numbers are requested, say 'Between ace and four, because the ace doesn't count, we are left with two or three.' If the spectator asks for three, you are fine, but if two is requested say 'That leaves us with three'. If the spectator asks for high numbers, the elimination works again, and you say that this leaves the low numbers. By this method you can always arrive at the card you first selected.

This trick can only be carried off with practice, and clear and quick thinking.

FAST FIND CARD TRICK

· · · · ☆ ☆ ☆ · · · ·

Finding a chosen card quickly, without fuss or bother, can often be a difficult task. The version which follows is not only cheeky in method but clever in performance.

Effect

A card is freely selected by a member of the audience, who then freely returns the card to any position in the pack. The performer immediately locates the spectator's chosen card.

Apparatus

A regular pack of cards and a pencil.

Set-up

Beforehand, and in secret, run a pencil line down one side of the pack; the line should be fairly light, but should be visible to you.

Working and Presentation

Fan the pack of cards, face-down, towards a spectator, and ask her to freely select a card. When the card has been removed and while it is being shown to members of the audience by the spectator, secretly turn the pack around before the selected card is returned. Because the pack has been reversed, the chosen card is the only card showing a pencil mark against the plain white edges of the rest of the pack. It is now an easy matter to break at that card and remove it to prove that it is indeed the chosen card.

LEFT In the set-up to this trick, mark the pack by running a pencil line lightly down one side of the pack.

LEFT In performance, secretly turn the pack round before the spectator replaces the card. The chosen card is immediately apparent by its mark.

FIFTY-TWO THOUGHTS

· · · · ☆ ☆ ☆ · · · ·

As a clever card worker or possessor of amazing memory, you will
gain much credit when performing this trick.

Effect

A pack of cards is shuffled and handed to the performer who, one after the other, reveals the names of all 52 cards.

Apparatus

A regular pack of cards, a borrowed one if so wished.

Working and Presentation

Have the pack of cards shuffled by a member of the audience, reclaim the pack and memorize the top facing card. Place the cards behind your back, both hands assisting, and secretly cut the pack, approximately in central position. Secretly place the two sections back to back so that one stock of cards is facing one way and one stock the other. Bring out the pack face on, so that the audience clearly sees the front card. This card is the one that you have already glimpsed and remembered; announce its name. At the same time glance at the card now facing you. Replace the pack behind your back, remove and discard the top card and secretly reverse the pack once more. Bring the pack out to the front again; the card now facing the audience – appearing to be the one beneath the card which has just been divined and discarded – is the second card you looked at. Announce its name.

Follow the same procedure until all the cards have been named and discarded, reversing the pack each time behind the back so that the next card comes into view. The audience is never aware that half the pack is facing the performer during the presentation.

LEFT The performer's view of the secretly cut and reversed portion of the pack.

CLEAN CUT

· · · · ☆ ☆ ☆ · · · ·

Another card effect that uses a table knife.

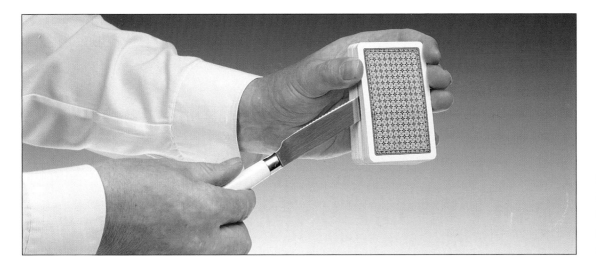

LEFT Insert the knife blade into the secretly buckled pack to reveal the selected card.

Effect

A spectator is asked to freely select a card from the pack. The pack is cut into two portions, the spectator's card being placed between the halves, and the pack is well shuffled. Next, a table knife is shown. The performer holds the pack in his left hand, and with the right hand, forces the knife into the pack. When a spectator takes the pack and removes the uppermost portion, and then looks at the card beneath the blade of the knife, it is the chosen one.

Apparatus

A regular pack of cards and a table knife.

Working and Presentation

The secret of this card trick is simple, but a little misdirection is required. Have a card freely selected from the pack, and ask the spectator to display it to the audience. While the card is being displayed, secretly buckle the pack, squeezing with the right hand so that a slight curve occurs. Ask the spectator to cut the pack and replace the chosen card, returning it to the top of the bottom pile. This brings about a definite break in the pack and, no matter how well shuffled, it is possible to locate the chosen card.

Hold the pack in the left hand and the knife in the right. Force the knife through the slight gap in the pack so that when it is parted by the spectator the chosen card lies beneath the blade.

It is best to perform this effect amid other card tricks, so that in due course the buckled pack regains its shape.

★ MISDIRECTION ★

Misdirection is the art of drawing the spectators' attention in a certain direction at the critical moments – to flourish an empty hand in which an object is believed to be concealed, while secretly disposing of the article with the other hand. You may have seen a magician produce a billiard ball in his or her right hand, holding it up in the air for all to see, while at the same time carefully using his left hand to steal away a live dove from a pocket, ready for the next startling effect. Ask someone to look up in the air, and they will. Hold something in your hand and elevate it into the air for everyone to see, and their eyes should follow; that is misdirection. Get ready to steal something away from your person and in comes your attractive assistant, and all eyes turn to her. Misdirection assists magicians in obtaining the very best in magic.

Misdirection, I believe, can also be executed by word alone, a certain patter line, even a change of tone in the voice. The spectator or audience perceives this, and attention is diverted away from the manoeuvre you want to keep secret.

IN THE DARK

· · · · · ☆ ☆ ☆ · · · · ·

The audience will certainly be in the dark while watching this
rather puzzling card miracle.

Effect

A pack of cards is well shuffled. A spectator
is asked to freely select one card, but is told
not to look at its identity at this stage of the
procedure. To make it even more difficult,
the room lights are switched off so that
everything is in the dark. The chosen card is
placed face down onto the palm of the
spectator's hand. Dramatically, the performer
announces the name of the chosen card. The
experiment is repeated another two times
with similar startling results.

Apparatus

A regular pack of cards.

Working and Presentation

This effect is best performed in a series of
other card tricks. When the time comes,
secretly palm off three cards from the pack,
note their values and pocket them (see
Chapter 1 for various ways of palming cards).

In performance ask the spectator to select
a card but not to look at its suit or value at
this stage. The lights are switched off and

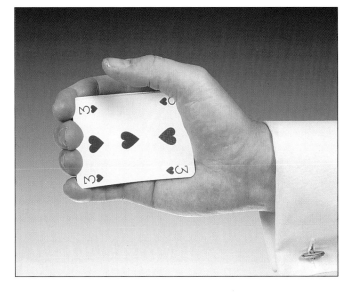

LEFT The trick to this
card effect is to
secretly palm off
three cards from the
pack.

you take the card. In replacing the card onto
the palm of the spectator's hand, secretly
exchange the chosen card with one from the
pocket. Of course, this is all done in the
dark; unknown to the audience, a clever
switch has been made.

Announce the value and suit of the chosen
card. When the lights are switched on, and
the spectator reverses the card, he finds it is
the one which you have divined.

To avoid confusing the unwanted cards
with the palmed cards within the pocket, a
simple method of keeping them apart is to
have a folded pocket handkerchief acting as
a divider. Cards that are secretly placed into
the pocket go on one side of the handkerchief and those that are being removed, on
the other. This means that the card effect can
be repeated several times without any
complications arising.

PRINTER'S DREAM

· · · · ☆ ☆ ☆ · · · ·

A printer's dream comes true in this effect.

Effect

The performer fans a pack of plain white cards showing the cards are really blank on both sides. When he next fans the cards towards the audience, the pack appears to be fully printed.

Apparatus

Believe it or not, a genuine pack of cards is required for this near miracle, although it is important that it should display indices on only two corners of each card and not four – some packs have the indices printed on all four corners. It is also important that the back design does not bleed off, but has a wide white border.

Also required are two double-blank playing cards (white on both sides). The performer can obtain these either from a complete pack from a magic dealer, or make them up by neatly covering the front and back of each of the jokers with white contact adhesive material.

Set-up

Have one double-blank card at the top of the pack and one at the bottom. Place the pack carefully into its case and you are all set to begin the performance.

Working and Presentation

Remove the cards from the case and 'reverse fan' the pack. In other words, instead of fanning the pack as normal, from left to right, fan from right to left. The reverse fan covers the indices, and with the blank white card on the face of the pack the whole pack appears to be blank. Because the pattern on the backs of the cards has a wide white border around each one, the other face of the fan appears blank, too.

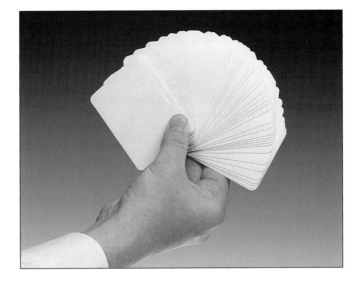

LEFT Reverse fan the specially selected pack from right to left. With the secret addition of a dummy blank white card on both the top and the bottom of the pack, the cards appear to be totally blank.

LEFT Fan the same pack as normal, from left to right, to reveal normal printed cards. (Note the pack is printed with the indices in two corners only.)

Square up the pack, turn it face downwards, and remove the blank card from what is now the bottom of the pack. Show this card on both sides just as an additional flourish to convince the audience that each card is blank on both sides. Now replace this card, but on top of the other double-blank card, which is already in top position.

Now turn the pack over, wave your hand over the front card, and it appears to be printed. Fan the pack, but this time in the usual manner – from left to right – showing that the faces of the cards are now printed.

Cut the pack so that the two blank white cards are now approximately in the middle, then fan the cards to show the printed back designs. Be careful not to fully expose the two blank cards in the middle.

You have just printed a complete pack of blank cards by magic!

★ FORCING CARDS ★

There will be times when the performer may have to 'force' a card or cards onto a spectator to achieve some effects. While many methods rarely rely upon sleight of hand or dexterity, some do. For the benefit of the general magician wishing to learn these important techniques, the most practical have been included here.

★ FALSE SHUFFLING ★

From time to time you will rely upon what is known as false shuffling when performing some of the card effects described in this section. There are several methods of false shuffling — that is shuffling the pack in a convincing manner yet leaving all or most of the cards undisturbed. Here are two variations:

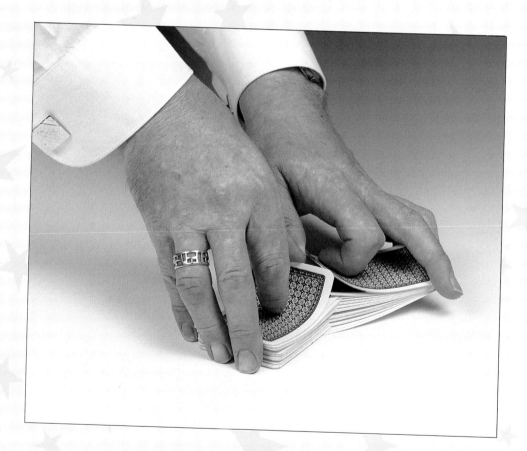

ABOVE To keep just one card at the top of the pack, the cards can be riffle-shuffled — the top card always remains in top position.

1 To keep several cards at the top of the pack in their original sequence, bring the top section from the rear to the front.

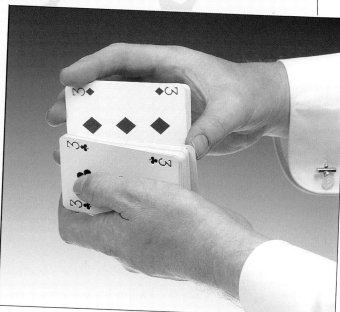

3 . . . return the cards at the back of this section to the top again. Repeat the procedure.

2 Drop some of the cards at the front of the top section into the other hand, but . . .

4 The topmost cards will always remain on top of the pack.

THE FAMOUS FAN FORCE
• • • • ☆ ☆ ☆ • • • • •

Effect

This force is probably the most convincing of all, simply because the pack is fanned and a spectator is asked to take a card. It eliminates unnecessary counts or covering the pack with a handkerchief, for example. Fairness and simplicity register firmly in the minds of the audience.

Apparatus

A pack of cards.

Set-up

The card required for forcing should be at the top of the pack. If false shuffled (see above), retain the card in top position.

Working and Presentation

Cut the pack so that the top card is now approximately in the centre, but under your control – use the little finger of the left hand to create a tiny break marking its position. This break position must be controlled throughout the movements which follow.

Approach the spectator, advancing slowly. Start fanning the cards, face-down, from the right to the left, peeling off cards as required. Watch for the spectator's reaction, his hand coming forwards to take a card. As his hand moves forwards to grasp one, either slow down or speed up the procedure so that the right card reaches his fingertips at the right time, without him realizing the selection is under your control. Such actions must be smooth and appear to look casual and fair, for as the cards flow from one hand to the other you are responsible for the judgement of your movements.

Should the spectator pass the planned card, quickly rush through the pack to the end, quipping that the spectator must be decisive, and start the procedure again.

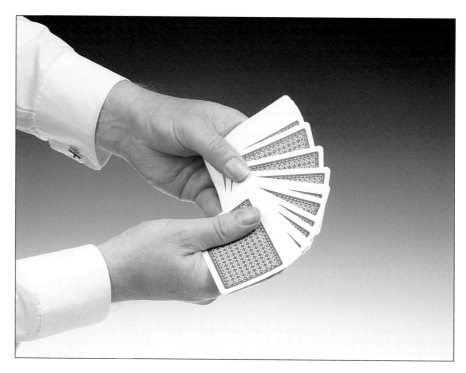

1 Slowly fan the cards from right to left as you approach the spectator.

2 Have the controlled card ready as the spectator is about to select.

3 Force the controlled card into the spectator's hand as he or she reaches forwards.

IN THE PALM OF YOUR HAND
· · · · ☆ ☆ ☆ · · · ·

Students who would like to resort to sleight-of-hand methods to accomplish a card force may well appreciate this one. Study the sleight-of-hand techniques using card palms in Chapter 1 before attempting this trick.

Apparatus

A pack of cards.

Set-up

The card to be forced is on top of the pack.

Working and Presentation

False shuffle the pack, keeping the top card in top position. Grip the pack between the fingers and thumb of the right hand; in transferring it from the right hand to the left, allow the top card to pivot upwards into palm position. This is executed as the pack is placed on the table. Keep the palmed card in a natural hand position.

Ask a spectator to cut the pack into two piles. This being done, with the right hand (containing the concealed palmed card) casually reach over to lift up the bottom section of the cut. In doing so, add the palmed card to the top of this section of cards. Transfer these cards into the left hand once again. Ask the spectator to remove the card where the cut was made, and to reverse it, revealing its identity.

The beauty of this method is that a borrowed pack can be used, and that there is no previous preparation required.

CLIP-IT

· · · · ☆ ☆ ☆ · · · ·

This card force has been devised specially for this book. The clip-it force relies on simplicity and the use of a common office accessory – a paper-clip.

LEFT In the set-up, place a paper-clip on the bottom edge of the card you intend to force.

Effect

The performer announces the name and value of the card he intends to force. The pack is fanned out, face-down, to a member of the audience, who freely selects a card, but does not look at it. A paper-clip is handed to the spectator, and he is requested to slide it onto the top edge of that card, so as to mark it out. The spectator replaces the marked card somewhere in the middle of the pack, and the performer cuts the cards several times.

The performer recaps on what has been done so far and then fans out the pack bringing to the attention of the audience the clipped card. When the card is removed and finally displayed, it is the card that the performer intended to force.

Apparatus

A pack of cards and two paper-clips.

Set-up

Beforehand, decide which card to force, and onto that particular card attach one of the two paper-clips, in central position along the bottom edge. Place the card somewhere in the middle of the pack, with the paper-clip facing into the hand, so that the top edges of the fanned pack will appear genuine and unmarked.

Working and Presentation

Ask a spectator to select a card from a pack fanned out, face-down. Keep the selected card face-down and ask the spectator to slip a paper-clip onto the middle of the top edge and return it to the pack.

In closing up the pack, give it a half-turn, bringing the opposite ends towards the audience. Cut the pack several times and fan the pack again so that the audience can clearly see that one card has a paper-clip on it – this appears to be the one which the spectator clipped. Remove this and hand it to the spectator, discarding the remainder of the pack. The spectator then reveals that it is, indeed, the card you intended to force.

Should the spectator just happen to pick your clipped card – unlikely, but possible – you have a miracle on your hands. Simply remove it, revealing the paper-clip attached to it, and that it is the *only* card which displays such a clip, later proving this to be the correctly predicted card.

HAT FORCE

· · · · · ☆ ☆ ☆ · · · ·

Magicians are known for pulling things out of a hat and this card force is no exception.

Effect

The blindfolded performer reaches inside a hat, and from the well-shuffled pack of cards removes the chosen card.

Apparatus

A pack of cards. Although a hat is mentioned, any container such as a small box or cylindrical container can be used.

Set-up

The secret is simple; conceal the card to be forced in the right sleeve of your jacket.

Working and Presentation

In performance the shuffled pack is placed inside the hat or container. Announce the name of the chosen card, and either ask to be blindfolded or simply turn away. Hold the hat in the left hand or place it on a table, and as you reach inside to make your selection, allow the card secreted in the right sleeve to drop into the hat. This move is executed under cover of the hat itself. With this card loose from the others, it is a simple matter to pull it out, and reveal it to be the predicted card.

ABOVE In performance, allow the chosen card, previously concealed in the right-hand jacket sleeve, to secretly drop into the hat.

CRISS-CUT FORCE

· · · · ☆ ☆ ☆ · · · ·

Effect

A spectator makes a free cut in a pack of cards and the performer correctly predicts the card beneath the cut.

Apparatus

A pack of cards.

Set-up

Beforehand, secretly note the top card.

Working and Presentation

Request a spectator to cut the pack somewhere in the centre, and then to place his stack of cards beside the other. State that you will mark the cut by laying the cut stack across the bottom stack. Some misdirection is now required; you could, for example, flourish an envelope containing your prediction, if you have not already announced this at the start of the trick. The misdirection will divert attention from the next move. To 'mark the cut', actually cross the *bottom* stack on top of the *cut* stack. Ask the spectator to reveal his cut by lifting the top stack and reversing the card immediately below it. This card will be the top card you noted before the performance and predicted.

BELOW The spectator's cut is marked by crossing the stacks. However, unknown to the audience, the stacks have been swopped one for the other, so that the predicted card takes the position of the cut card.

UNDERCOVER

• • • • ☆ ☆ ☆ • • • •

This is a popular force among beginners.

Effect

Again the performer correctly predicts at which card a spectator will make a free cut of a shuffled pack. The twist here is that the cut is made under cover of a pocket handkerchief.

Apparatus

A pack of regular cards and a pocket handkerchief.

Set-up

Secretly note the top card of the pack.

Working and Presentation

As you hand the pack to a spectator to inspect and shuffle, secretly palm off the top *two* cards of the pack with the left hand. Take the pack from the spectator and place it in the left hand so that the palmed cards are now face-up on the bottom of the pack. Display a pocket handkerchief and drape it over the pack.

Ask a spectator to cut the pack through the material of the handkerchief, but not to lift the cut stack away completely. With the right hand take hold of the cut stack and as you draw this top stack and the handkerchief away, reverse the bottom stack in your left hand under cover of the handkerchief. The original top card of the pack is now face-down and on top of the bottom stack. The spectator now reverses this card to reveal the cut and it is the card you originally predicted. The card immediately below it is also face-down, concealing the fact that the rest of the bottom stack is now face-up.

LEFT Take hold of the spectator's cut portion of the pack – the two palmed cards are lying face-up on the bottom of the pack.

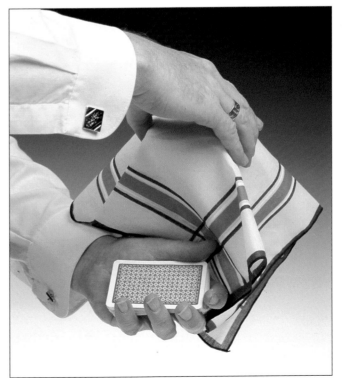

LEFT As you draw the cut stack away, secretly reverse the bottom stack under cover of the handkerchief. The two reversed cards at the bottom of the pack are now on top of the bottom stack. The predicted card now takes the position of the cut card.

CLASSICS OF CONJURING

Every magician should spend time to perfect some of the classics of magic – tried and tested effects that have become familiar to audiences all over the world. Some students make the mistake of passing over this section of a magician's repertoire, including old favourites such as the multiplying balls, the six card repeat and the time-honoured rabbit from a hat. However, they remain as popular today as on the day they were first introduced, especially when combined with imaginative new routines.

THE CHINESE LINKING RINGS
☆ ☆ ☆

This classic piece of magic is performed by magicians all over the world.

Effect

The Chinese Linking Rings brings about a series of visual moves linking and unlinking solid metal rings. The effect has, in the past, been performed silently with a musical background, but can be presented with amusing patter. Many different routines have evolved over the years, some using three rings, some four, five, eight and sixteen. The most usual version uses eight solid silver rings, all of which appear to be handled by members of the audience during the effect.

Apparatus

Although a professional set of linking rings can be bought from a magic dealer, it is possible for the individual to manufacture his or her own. If he is proficient in working with metal, he will be able to make the necessary apparatus.

You will need a set of eight rings, comprised of the following: two single rings; a set of two rings permanently linked together; a set of three rings permanently linked together; the 'key' ring (a ring with a gap).

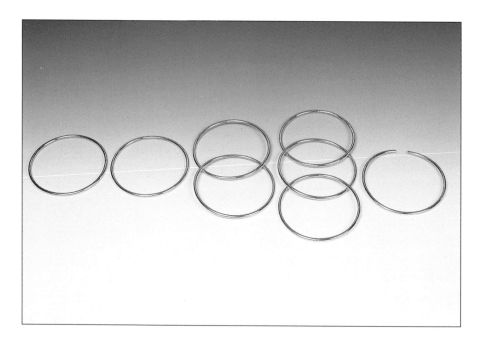

Set-up

Have the rings resting on a table or over the back of a chair. They should be set in this order, from the bottom of the stack: the key, one single, the chain of three, the chain of two and one single. It is important to pick up the set in this order.

Working and Presentation

The classic introduction: 'A trick from China, as old as magic itself, it is called the Chinese Linking Rings. Before your very eyes you will see these solid rings do incredible things. Ladies and gentlemen, eight solid steel rings. Let me count them.'

☆ COUNTING THE RINGS ☆

1 In counting the rings, use the 'drop count'. Hold the rings in the left hand.

2 Allow the first single ring to drop from the others to be caught in the right hand. Lower this hand slightly so that the ring is separate from the others of the set.

3 Next, allow the two linked rings to drop singly into the awaiting right hand, which, as before, is lowered.

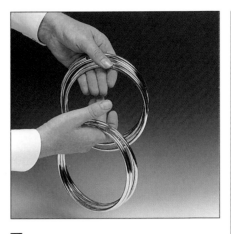

4 Similarly, drop the following three linked rings so that they appear to fall one at a time into the right hand. Finally, drop the second single ring and then lower the key ring. You have now apparently dropped and counted eight solid and separate rings.

5 Keep the rings in their original order when transferring them back to the left hand. The gap in the key ring is always to the top and covered by the thumb of the left hand during the presentation.

☆ LINKING TWO RINGS ☆

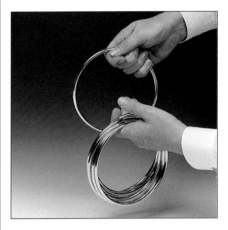

1 Remove from the front the first single ring with the right hand and 'crash' it against the others. Simultaneously, allow the first of the two linked rings to fall from the first finger of the left hand.

2 To the audience it appears that you have caused the first ring to penetrate the second. Remove the two linked rings to display a perfectly coupled pair and hand them to a spectator for a thorough examination.

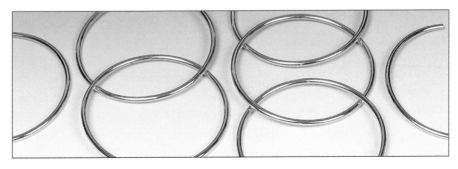

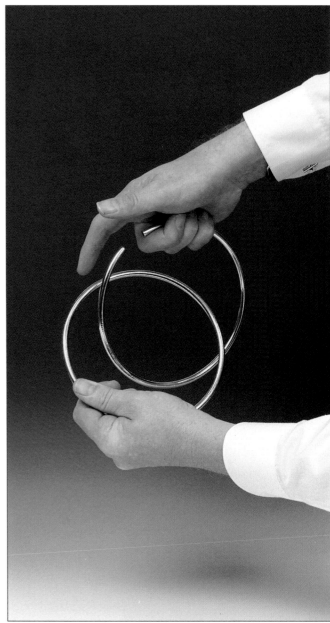

ABOVE In 'linking' three rings, the same procedure is followed as in the previous stage. The single ring is crashed against the set, and the first then the second rings from the linked set of three are allowed to drop.

☆ LINKING THREE RINGS ☆

Remove the loose single ring, still in front position, with the right hand, and again crash it against the front of the set. Allow the first of the set of three linked rings to drop and hang. Again crash the loose single ring against the others, so that the second of the set of three linked rings falls to make its appearance.

Take the hanging rings away from the set to show that three rings are now linked together and hand them to another spectator for examination.

☆ LINKING THE LAST TWO RINGS ☆

At this stage, you are left holding three single rings, one of which is the key. Place one of the solid single rings over the arm.

Holding the remaining solid ring and the key ring in both hands, rub them together, engaging the solid ring onto and over the key ring. The rubbing motion should continue for a short period even after the rings are actually linked together. Suddenly, allow the solid ring to drop so that it becomes linked to the other (the key).

ABOVE The last two rings – one solid, one the key – are simply linked by passing the solid ring over the gap in the key ring.

☆ CONFOUNDING THE AUDIENCE ☆

Turn to the first spectator holding the chain of two, and ask him to repeat your actions. Hold the two linked rings in front of the body, rub them together and ask the spectator to do the same with his two linked rings. Your rings become parted, but the rings held by the spectator will remain linked and cannot be separated.

Now remove the solid single ring from your arm, rub the three rings together, engaging the two solid rings onto the key ring. Gather together your set of three rings and ask the second spectator to repeat your actions. First, remove one loose ring. Alas, the spectator finds it impossible to do the same. Remove a second ring (the key) with the thumb covering the gap, and throw the third ring into the air to prove that all three are completely separate at this stage. The spectator's rings still remain linked. Link your three rings together again.

Ask the first spectator to hand over his set of two linked rings. Take these and rub them against your linked three. Under cover of the rubbing motion, link them all together forcing one of the set of two linked rings over the gap in the key. Grip the key ring so that the others hang from it.

In continuing the routine, take the chain of three linked rings from the second spectator and likewise place it alongside the others, forcing one over the key, as before.

In preparation for the final startling effect, display the entire set of rings, seven hanging from the uppermost ring (the key) gripped in the hand.

'Ladies and gentlemen, eight solid rings of steel. In my hands they have become as soft as jelly. But, let me prove once again that we have, just as we started with, eight solid separate rings.'

Holding the set high above your head and away from the body, you have reached the climax of the trick. Under cover, open the gap in the key ring so that the others auto-matically scatter – apparently all single again – to the floor, dropping the key ring last of all.

Although this classic effect and routine is easy to perform, a certain amount of practice, skill and dexterity are required to become proficient in handling the rings.

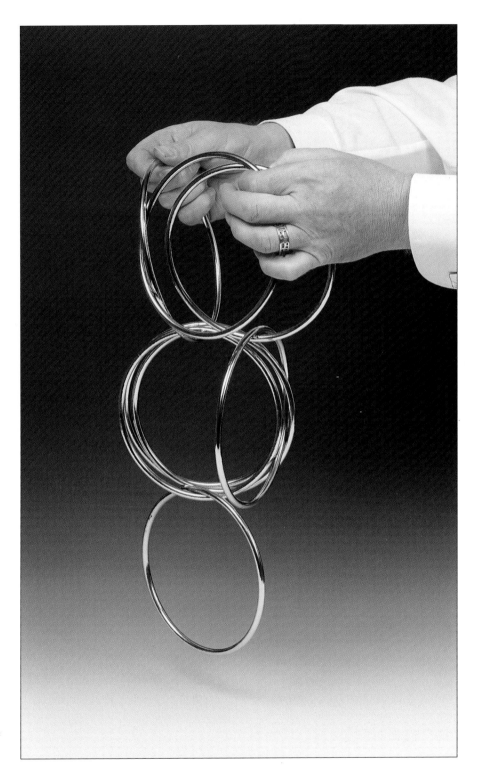

ABOVE In the penultimate stage of the trick, all eight rings are linked together.

THE MULTIPLYING BILLIARD BALLS

• • • • ☆ ☆ ☆ • • • •

Often sold in more advanced boxes of magic, this is usually one of the first tricks the beginner learns.

Effect

The performer reaches into the air; a red billiard ball materializes. It multiplies to two, to three and then to four, all four balls being displayed between the fingers. The balls can be made to vanish singly, transpose and reappear elsewhere, at will.

Apparatus

The set comprises three solid balls and one shell (a hollow half-ball). The shell is especially made to fit over any of the three balls. It is a good idea to paint the balls with red lacquer, as this colour allows audiences large and small to see the balls clearly during the performance. A silk handkerchief is also required.

Set-up

Place one ball, with the shell over it, in the right trouser pocket. Place the second ball inside the left trouser pocket. Place the third ball in the left jacket pocket with the silk handkerchief.

Working and Presentation

The pivoting move, on which this sequence relies, may at first seem awkward to the beginner, but constant practice, preferably in front of a mirror, will enable anyone to master these moves and present a polished performance.

☆ **PRODUCING TWO BILLIARD BALLS** ☆

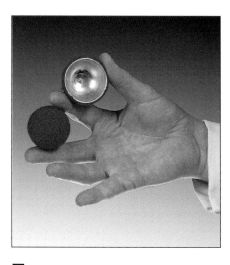

3 ... like this.

1 With the right hand casually resting in the right trouser pocket, palm the ball with the shell over it. Remove the hand from the pocket and pluck this ball out of the air to appear between the thumb and the first finger. Show it on both sides as one ball.

2 Lower the second finger of the right hand to pivot the solid ball out from the shell ...

4 To the audience you appear to be holding two solid balls.

☆ THE VANISH ☆

Raise the left hand as if to take away the ball gripped between the first and second fingers, but in fact use it as a shield to conceal the following move. Under cover make a clutching motion with the right hand, allowing the ball to pivot back inside the shell.

Withdraw the closed left fist, supposedly holding a ball, from the right hand, where one solid ball appears to remain, gripped between the thumb and first finger. Slowly open the left hand to reveal that it is empty.

☆ PRODUCING THREE BILLIARD BALLS ☆

Reach inside the left trouser pocket with the left hand, removing the planted ball. As you position this ball between the first and second fingers of the right hand, quickly pivot out the ball within the shell to be held between the second and third fingers. Three balls have now been magically produced.

☆ ANOTHER VANISH ☆

Shield the centre ball with the left hand, pretending to remove it from its position. As you appear to grasp it, pivot the ball back inside the shell.

This time pretend to place the ball, supposedly in the left hand, into your mouth. As your clenched fist moves up in front of your mouth, press the tongue against the side of the cheek so that it looks as if the mouth is holding the ball.

Show that the left hand is empty, and with the first finger push the 'bulge' inwards, as if swallowing the ball.

☆ PRODUCING FOUR BILLIARD BALLS ☆

Reach inside the left jacket pocket with the left hand and produce the ball planted there. Place it firmly between the third and fourth fingers of the right hand and show the three balls on both sides.

Produce the final fourth ball from within the shell, as before, using the pivoting action, so that it now takes its place between the first and second fingers.

☆ MORE VANISHES ☆

Vanish two balls as follows. Show the right hand holding the four balls. Shake your hand in the air and one ball appears to have vanished – you have pivoted the ball between the first and second fingers inside the shell, leaving three in view. Show both sides of the remaining balls to the audience.

With the left hand move the ball between the second and third fingers and reposition it between the first and second fingers of the right hand. Under cover of this move 'steal' away the ball from within the shell with the left hand – simply allow the ball to drop out of the shell and into the awaiting clenched fist. Make a second vanish with the right hand – pivoting the ball now held between the first and second fingers into the shell – and at the same time secretly pocket the unwanted ball from the left hand.

Now remove the ball from between the third and fourth fingers and place it between the first and second fingers. In doing this, again 'steal' away the ball from within the shell with the left hand as before.

☆ A QUICK TRANSPOSITION ☆

Drop the left hand, formed in a fist, beside the body, with the back of the hand towards the audience. Similarly, lower the right hand, containing what appear to be two solid balls, of which one is really the shell.

With a throwing motion of the right hand, vanish the solid ball held between the first and second fingers, secretly pivoting it inside the shell. Simultaneously, produce the palmed ball within the left hand – a rather neat transposition.

☆ HANDKERCHIEF VANISH ☆

Place this ball between the first and second fingers of the right hand and, under cover, steal away the one inside the shell.

Reach inside the left jacket pocket and remove the silk handkerchief; at the same time deposit the ball taken from the shell into the pocket. With the left hand hold the silk by one corner, draping it over both balls, and then reach beneath, supposedly to take one away. In fact, pivot the ball into the shell, and withdraw the left hand as if holding the ball.

Slowly open the fingers of the left hand to show the ball has vanished and then remove the handkerchief to show that only one ball remains in the right hand. Pocket the handkerchief; the remaining ball, together with the shell, can be vanished by any of the sleight-of-hand methods described in Chapter 1.

The routine should end, as it began, with the hands completely empty.

CUPS AND BALLS

· · · · ☆ ☆ ☆ · · · ·

Possibly the oldest trick in the world, the famous Cups and Balls has been performed in every country using all types of goblets or cups. Fakirs have performed the routine on the pavements, and in India one can still see the street magicians present it alongside their snake charming. Cups and Balls was presented in Victorian drawing rooms, and in France it is called 'Le Jeu des Goblets'.

Effect

The actual effect of the Cups and Balls varies from performer to performer, but to sum it up, balls vanish, appear, transpose and even change to fruits and vegetables, and in some cases, live chicks.

Apparatus

Although the routine can be presented with opaque beakers, it is best performed with the correct type of goblet. Magic dealers manufacture sets of three goblets in spun aluminium, brass and copper. Some are called 'dumpies' – a term given to the shape – while others look rather like beakers. All have a 'wall' around the mouth of each goblet, and all are made to stack on top of each other. Because of the walls, when the cups are stacked together, a similar amount of space is given between each so that a secreted ball can be hidden with ease. All three cups have a small indentation in their bottoms so that when each goblet is placed face down onto the table, a ball rests on top comfortably without rolling off.

The student may initially wish to follow the various moves described here using clear plastic tumblers. This means that the performer can practise, having a clearer view of the location of each ball.

You will need three goblets or opaque plastic beakers; four small sponge or cork balls; three larger sponge balls.

Set-up

Conceal the three large balls in the right trouser pocket and three of the small balls in the left trouser pocket. Place the fourth ball in one cup and stack the remaining two cups on top.

The entire set should be displayed as follows: the nesting cups should stand upright, mouths upwards, positioned to the left of your working area.

LEFT The beakers neatly stack one on top of another. The walls around the beakers prevent them from being pushed right into each other when stacked. The space created between two stacked beakers can be used to conceal a ball. The small indentation on the base of each beaker allows for a ball to balance there without falling off.

Working and Presentation
☆ THE GALLOP MOVE ☆

1 Display the cups. Pick them up in the left hand and show the nest mouth-on to the audience. With the right hand, take hold of the bottom cup ready to perform the gallop move, as follows.

2 Invert the bottom cup, containing the secreted ball, upon the table so that the ball secretly drops with it to lie underneath the cup.

3 Remove the two remaining cups from the stack one by one in a similar fashion, placing them in a line, mouth downwards, alongside the first one.

✫ THE PLACE-IN MOVE ✫

1 Move the left hand as if to take the ball from the right hand.

2 Then clench the left fist as if holding the ball. Secretly palm the ball in the right hand and point to the left hand to reinforce the dummy move.

✫ THE LOADING POSITION ✫

LEFT With the right hand (holding the palmed ball), lift the cup to reveal one or several balls. Tilt the top of the cup forwards so that the mouth of the cup comes into the palm of the right hand. Secretly load the palmed ball into the cup ready for the next effect.

✫ A TRANSPOSITION ✫

Remove a small ball, the first of three, from the left trouser pocket and hold it in the right hand. Appear to pass the ball from the right hand to the left hand, but actually retain it in the right – this is known as the place-in move (see **The Place-in Move** on this page). With the right hand (holding the concealed ball), lift the cup on the left, tilting it forwards towards the audience. Pretend to place the ball, supposedly in the left hand, under this cup – the ball actually remains concealed in the right hand.

Pointing to each cup, make the following announcement: 'Ladies and gentlemen, a transformation. Watch the ball travel from this cup to the one on the opposite side'. Lift the cup on the left and the audience clearly sees that it is empty. Lift the cup in the centre, which is also empty. In continuing the routine, lift the cup on the right with the right hand, tilting the top of the cup down towards the audience, to show that the ball has 'transferred'. While the audience's attention is diverted by this production, allow the ball concealed in the right hand to secretly drop into the mouth of the cup. This loading procedure is standard practice among magicians (see **The Loading Position** on this page). Execute the gallop move again, inverting the cup upon the table, with the secretly loaded ball remaining underneath the cup ready for the next effect.

✫ PRODUCING ONE BALL ✫

Take the ball now on view in the right hand and, again, supposedly place the ball in the left hand. 'Which cup do you wish the ball to reappear under, Madam?' you ask, peering at your clenched left hand. The spectator has a choice of three cups. Should she point to either the left or centre cup lift the cup of her choice with the right hand, tilting the top of the cup towards the audience, and release the palmed ball beneath, so that a ball suddenly appears at this position.

Should the spectator select the cup on the right, simply lift the cup to reveal the ball previously loaded at this position. However, since a ball must remain hidden beneath the right-hand cup ready for a further effect, load the ball palmed in the right hand into the cup as it is lifted to make the production. Execute the gallop move again, the mouth of the cup hitting the surface of the table and concealing the loaded ball inside. You are now ready to perform a penetration.

☆ FURTHER PRODUCTIONS ☆

Using the gallop move, display the cups once again upon the table, with the secreted ball now concealed under the centre cup. 'Vanish' the visible ball within the hands, using any of the sleight-of-hand methods described in Chapter 1. Actually retain it in the palm of the right hand. Lift the centre cup with the right hand, showing that the ball has made its appearance beneath. While the audience

☆ A PENETRATION ☆

2 Place the centre cup then the left-hand cup on the stack, crashing them down as if to assist in a dramatic penetration.

1 With the hidden ball underneath the right cup, you are ready to present a penetration. Place the visible ball on top of the right-hand cup.

3 Lift the entire stack of cups to reveal the loaded ball. To the audience, the ball placed on top of the right-hand cup appears to have penetrated its base to fall to the table. (Continue with *Further Productions*.)

is appreciating this fact, allow the palmed ball to drop inside this cup which is in the loading position – mouth upwards into the palm of the hand, ready to receive the ball. Place the cup, using the gallop move, over the ball just produced.

Remove a second ball from the left trouser pocket and vanish it. The individual will have preferences in the methods used for such vanishes, but basically the right hand always secretly retains the ball. Lift the centre cup to reveal the 'vanished' ball, together with the first one. With the cup gripped in the right hand, load the palmed ball inside ready for the third and final production of the smaller balls, and invert the cup over the two balls on the table. In the same way, remove a third ball from the left trouser pocket, vanish it and make it 'reappear' under the centre cup.

Casually put the right hand into the right trouser pocket and discard the palmed ball. Simultaneously, obtain one of the three larger balls in the finger-palm position. While you

do this, arrange the three smaller balls with the left hand so that they are neatly displayed, one on top of each of the cups.

☆ TIP-OFF LOADING MOVE ☆

This move is executed three times to vanish the three small balls, and produce the three large balls, one under each cup. Grip the base of the cup on the right with the right hand (holding the large palmed ball) and tilt it over towards the audience allowing the small ball, resting on the top, to fall into the waiting cupped left hand. This gesture simply creates the impression that here is a practical way of dropping the ball from the top of the cup into the hand, without touching it.

While you are presenting this flourish, allow the large ball concealed in the right hand to drop inside the cup. This is the same loading position used previously. Immediately tilt this cup back so that it returns mouth down once again.

Take the smaller ball in the right hand and

put it in the right trouser pocket. Under cover, finger-palm the second large ball from this pocket while pointing to the centre cup with the left hand, and in particular to the ball resting on it. Load the large ball inside the cup as before, and again pocket the small ball. In the same way, palm and load the third and final large ball inside the left cup. In pocketing the last of the three small balls, secretly gather all three together and push them securely under the top lining of the trouser pocket.

Announce to the audience that all three balls will vanish from the pocket to reappear under the cups. Reach inside the trouser pocket, withdrawing the lining to show that it is completely empty. All three balls have completely vanished. Lift the cups one by one, to reveal that not only have the three balls reappeared under the cups but have increased in size! The set of goblets and the balls can be thoroughly examined by members of the audience, if wished.

RABBIT FROM A HAT
· · · · ☆ ⭐ ☆ · · · ·

The appearance of a white rabbit from a top hat has been the mascot of the magician's craft and all magicians worthy of their salt should be able to perform this classic conjuring feat.

Effect

On the magician's table rests a black top hat. The performer takes it between his hands and displays it inside and out, even allowing a spectator or two to examine it if wished. A wave of the magic wand and the rabbit makes its surprising appearance.

Apparatus

The first thing you will need is a rabbit. These come in all shapes and sizes, but it is most important that it should be of the dwarf variety (the Netherland Dwarf is ideal) for the effect to work.

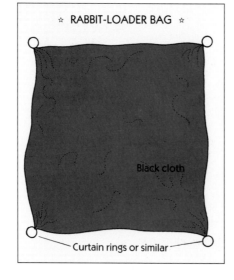

☆ RABBIT-LOADER BAG ☆

Black cloth

Curtain rings or similar

A top hat. There are two varieties available: the solid variety which does not fold, or the opera hat, which does.

A table which has a cloth drape covering it. A hook or nail should be hammered onto the back of the table in a central position. A magic wand.

A specially made 'rabbit-loader' bag. As illustrated, this consists of a square of black cloth which has a ring attached to each of the corners. This piece of cloth should be large enough to hold the rabbit firmly, by bringing up all four corners and transforming it into a bag.

Set-up

With the rabbit already inside the bag, place the four rings at the corners onto the hook or nail at the rear of the table. Since the table has a cloth drape, it is impossible for the audience to see the bag from the front.

The top hat should already be on the table, open mouth downward, and towards the back in approximately central position, just in front of where the load bag is concealed. Put the magic wand in the left jacket pocket.

Working and Presentation

Turn the hat upside down so that the mouth of the hat is now uppermost. Now remove the hat from the table. The reason for this is two-fold: first, to show that the hat is empty, and second, to show the audience that the table top is clear.

Display the hat to all, making a special point of showing that there is nothing inside it. Should you be using a folding opera hat, collapse it as additional proof to the audience that it is indeed empty.

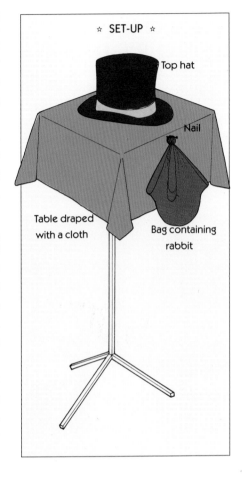

☆ SET-UP ☆

Top hat

Nail

Table draped with a cloth

Bag containing rabbit

Replace the hat on the table, in the original position, mouth downward. Take the magic wand from the pocket with the left hand and flourish in the air. You introduce this misdirection so that the right hand, in the act of lifting the hat away from the table, can execute the secret loading of the rabbit into the hat. This is done in one smooth, swift action.

With the right hand, lift the brim of the hat – the part of the brim lying towards the back of the table and pivot it over from back position towards the front. At the same time, disengage the rings from the hook at the rear with the thumb, so the load bag containing the rabbit automatically swings inside the hat. The weight of the rabbit makes this action quite easy to perform.

Once the load bag is inside the hat, tap the hat with the magic wand, release the rings, and the rabbit will free itself to make its appearance. The now flat piece of cloth is hidden within the interior of the hat. You have produced the proverbial magic rabbit from a top hat – follow that!

1 Display the hat to the audience to prove that it is empty, and replace it centrally towards the rear of the table, mouth downwards.

2 Lift the hat by the brim so that the top of the hat is tipped towards the audience. Slip the thumb of the same hand through the curtain rings and swing the bag into the open mouth of the hat and release it.

3 Place the hat on the table mouth up, and the rabbit, freed from the bag, makes its surprise appearance.

THE FAMOUS CUT AND RESTORED ROPE

· · · · · ☆ ☆ ☆ · · · · ·

Magicians have been cutting and restoring ropes for more years than I can possibly remember, as this is regarded as one of the greatest of all the classics of magic. This version is perhaps one of the simplest, and the preset arrangement provided makes for easier handling.

Effect

A length of soft white rope is doubled up, severed in the centre, shown as two pieces, and then magically restored to its original whole state.

Apparatus

A length of soft white rope; it is best to use magicians' rope, which is manufactured without the usual central core. A small loop of similar rope is also required. The ends of this short length can either be sewn together or bound with adhesive tape. A pair of sharp scissors. It is important to wear a watch and a jacket in this version.

Set-up

Push the ends of the loop of rope under the watch-strap so that the loop lies against the inner wrist. The cuff of the jacket covers this arrangement. Have the scissors and the length of rope on the table in front of you.

Working and Presentation

Display the length of rope by tugging it between the hands to prove it is one strong piece. Furthermore, allow a spectator to examine it. Hold the rope suspended in the left hand. With the right hand, locate the middle of the rope, and double the length up. As the looped portion of the doubled rope is brought up into the left hand, pull away the secreted loop of rope from the watch-strap and bring it up into the left hand. To the audience it appears that the centre of the length of rope is protruding

1 With the dummy loop secretly tucked into the watch-strap against the inner wrist, display the length of rope to the audience.

from your clenched left hand. Pick up the scissors with the right hand, and, with one definite cut, sever the dummy loop centrally. Then state that you will trim the ends of the rope, and proceed to do this, allowing the bits to fall to the floor. With the centre of the genuine rope still clenched within the left hand, simply blow on the rope and show that it is miraculously restored.

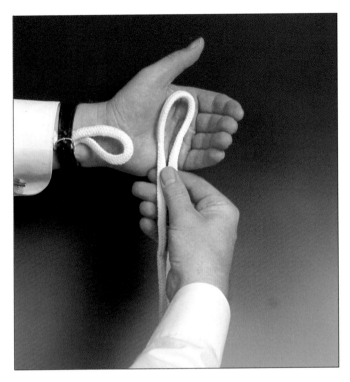

2 Locate the centre of the rope with the right hand, double it up and bring the looped portion into the left hand.

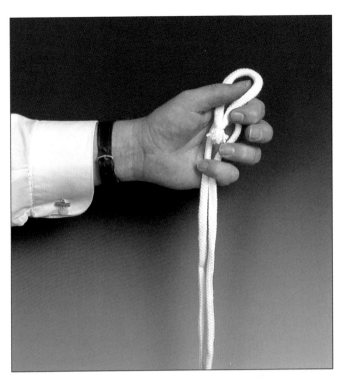

4 . . . bring it up through the fingers of the left hand.

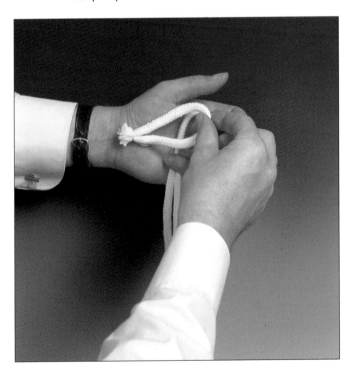

3 Secretly withdraw the dummy loop from the watch-strap and . . .

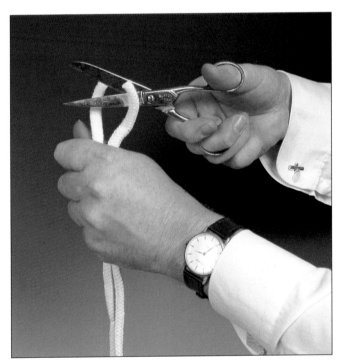

5 It is impossible for the audience to detect that this loop is not part of the original length of rope. Cut the dummy loop.

THE CLASSIC EGG BAG

· · · · · ☆ ☆ ☆ · · · ·

The famous Egg Bag trick was a feature of Arnold de Biere's music hall act; it was also a hit in the show *How's Tricks* presented by Australian-born Les Levante.
The trick lends itself to comedy presentation and can be performed at close quarters without detection. Furthermore, during the routine a number of magical things happen and there is plenty of audience participation involved.

Effect

A flat cloth bag is shown to the audience from all sides, inside and out – the bag appears to be empty, yet moments later an egg appears inside. The egg is made to vanish, reappear and finally find its way into a spectator's pocket.

Apparatus

A specially made cloth bag. The bag is faked so that while it has an inside and an outside, there is a secret pocket on one of the inside faces. This pocket has an opening towards the bottom. It is there both to conceal the egg and then later to allow the egg to drop into the bag proper.

You also require an imitation egg which can be made of plastic or wood. Some rubber joke eggs, available from joke and novelty stores, are ideal for this purpose. Experience has shown that a blown egg is not suitable for this presentation.

Set-up

Conceal the faked egg inside the secret pocket in the bag.

Working and Presentation

Lift the bag from the table, show both sides, then turn it inside out. To do this, grip the egg through the material of the bag as you turn the bag inside out. The egg will stay inside the bag during this procedure and all looks quite convincing – you appear to be holding an ordinary cloth bag. However, when showing the inside of the bag, always keep the side with the pocket towards the body and away from the audience. Turn the bag right side out again and you are ready to start the routine.

LEFT The classic egg bag seen right side out.

LEFT Now inside out, the secret pocket can be seen. Always keep this face of the bag towards you when displaying the classic egg bag.

Announce that you will produce an egg from the empty bag, using the magic word 'Eggstraordinary'. Say the magic word and place the empty right hand inside the bag. At the time time, release the left hand's grip of the egg through the material of the bag allowing the egg to drop out of its secret pocket into the bag. With a flourish, withdraw the right hand to reveal the egg.

Replace the egg inside the bag and ask a selected spectator to shout out the magic word 'Eggstraordinary'. This being done, invert the bag. Of course, nothing falls out because, in turning the bag mouth downwards towards the floor, the egg automatically drops into the pocket. The egg appears to have vanished. However, to make it even more convincing, turn the bag inside out as before, showing the inside to be empty and then bring the bag back to its original position. Now place the empty right hand inside the bag and reproduce the egg, showing it to the audience.

Next, put the egg back inside the bag, utter the magic word, and swish the right hand around inside the bag. Pretend to remove the egg, gripping the fist closed, and further pretend to secrete it under the left armpit. Continue with the presentation. Turn the bag inside out and back again showing that the egg has completely vanished, and when cries of 'it's under your arm' are heard, ignore them at first. Eventually, lift the right arm, showing that the egg is not there. The audience is not impressed. Lift the left arm showing that the egg is not there either. Then hold the bag open in both hands, and ask the spectator to reach inside and bring out the egg, which he does.

This could well be the climax of the effect but the more adventurous magician may wish to add something extra to give the routine a sting in the tail. Ask the spectator to open up the side pocket of the jacket he is wearing; tip the egg inside, or so it appears to the audience. In fact, when the bag is tilted, the egg rolls into the secret pocket and stays there. Tip the bag, mouth towards the floor, to prove that it is empty.

Turn the bag inside out with mouth upwards, so that the egg falls out of the pocket and into the right hand. Palm the egg in this hand and casually take it away while misdirecting attention towards the spectator's pocket. Ask if he still has the egg; the spectator reaches inside his pocket to find that the egg has mysteriously vanished. Look inside the spectator's pocket too and agree, but as this is being done, secretly drop the palmed egg into the pocket.

Pretend to try and make the egg reappear back inside the bag but without success. Try again and reach inside to bring out what you call an invisible egg, holding it between the fingers and thumb of the right hand.

Make a movement as if to toss the egg into the spectator's pocket. Ask the spectator to remove the egg from his pocket himself and drop it inside the bag, completing the routine.

20TH-CENTURY SILKS

· · · · ☆ ☆ ☆ · · · ·

Ask any practising magician to explain the working details of this trick and he will immediately know, for 20th-Century Silks has become a classic magical effect.

Effect

Two purple silk handkerchiefs are displayed and knotted together. A third silk of contrasting colour is shown and vanished, only to reappear tied and knotted between the other two.

Apparatus

A special set of silk handkerchiefs. This consists of a bag made from a purple silk square folded diagonally and sewn around the open edges, leaving a small opening at the top corner, as illustrated.

A purple silk handkerchief to match the above; a yellow silk handkerchief; and a yellow handkerchief to match the above but with a purple corner.

Set-up

Take the particoloured silk square and knot the yellow corner, diagonally opposite the purple one, to the open corner of the silk bag. Tuck the yellow handkerchief (with the purple corner) inside the purple silk bag, allowing the purple corner to protrude. The handkerchief is hidden inside during the presentation. Gather together the other two handkerchiefs so it appears that only three are being used.

Working and Presentation

First, pick up the two purple silks (one of which is the bag) and knot one corner of the purple silk to the false purple corner protruding from the silk bag. Tuck both silk handkerchiefs into a clear tumbler, with their corners hanging over the edge. Display the yellow silk handkerchief and make it vanish. Some performers use cones, boxes, tubes, etc to facilitate such a vanish, but the trouser

☆ APPARATUS ☆

Yellow silk square

Particoloured silk square

Purple silk square

Purple silk bag

☆ SET-UP ☆

Purple corner of particoloured silk protrudes from open corner

Purple silk bag

Particoloured silk concealed inside bag

LEFT The 'yellow' silk (actually the particoloured silk) miraculously appears knotted between the two purple silks.

pocket is just as effective. Place the silk handkerchief inside the pocket, and after uttering some magic words, pull out the lining of the pocket to show the vanish. The handkerchief has, in fact, been pushed up into the top section of the pocket. When the lining is turned out, the handkerchief is secured there and out of view.

Coming back to the silk handkerchiefs inside the tumbler, take the unattached corner of the standard purple silk and pull it away to show that the missing yellow silk has miraculously reappeared now firmly tied between the other two.

THE INEXHAUSTIBLE BOX

· · · · ☆ ☆ ☆ · · · ·

A classic piece of magical apparatus, this box is so unique that it is still being used by magicians worldwide.

Effect

The performer displays all sides of a square, lidded box and then tilts it forward and lifts the lid, allowing the spectators to see inside. Although the box is apparently empty, the magician proceeds to produce numerous items, even livestock, from inside the box. The box can be shown to be empty between each production.

Apparatus

The box is made with a pivoting load chamber which allows it to be shown on all sides including the base. The load chamber operates when the box is tilted over from back to front, so the top of the box faces the audience.

Set-up

Place as many items as required in the load chamber, and position the chamber inside the box at the start.

Working and Presentation

2 Tilt it forward towards the audience and lift the lid to display the inside.

3 The back view shows a rabbit in the concealed load chamber which now protrudes from the back of the box.

4 Position the box upright again and produce the rabbit from the top of the box.

1 Show the box on all sides.

UNEQUAL ROPES

· · · · · ☆ ☆ ☆ · · · · ·

Of all the rope tricks popular with audiences, Unequal Ropes is
probably one of the best.

Effect

The performer displays three different lengths
of rope: one very short, one medium length
and a long piece; side by side their differences are apparent.

The ends of the ropes are brought up to
meet the opposite ends, and while the
magician states that the three lengths are
now the same, the audience clearly sees that
the centres are not. The magician takes the
ends of the ropes in each hand and magically 'stretches' them, so that all three become
the same length. Furthermore, the lengths are
counted singly, proving the point.

The ends of the ropes are once again
placed end to end, blown onto, and mysteriously return to their original lengths, one
short, one medium and one long.

Apparatus

Three different lengths of rope. The ropes
must be identical in appearance and colour,
but there should be a short piece, a medium
piece twice as long as the short piece and a
long piece three times as long as the short
piece. Keep the three lengths knotted together ready for the presentation – you will
avoid losing one of them at the vital moment.

Working and Presentation

1 Unknot the ropes and display them to
the audience in order of length to
emphasize their differences: first, hold up
the short length and then place it in the
left hand; then the medium length,
placing it in the left hand to the right of
the short length; and finally the long
length, placing it in the left hand to the
right of the medium length.

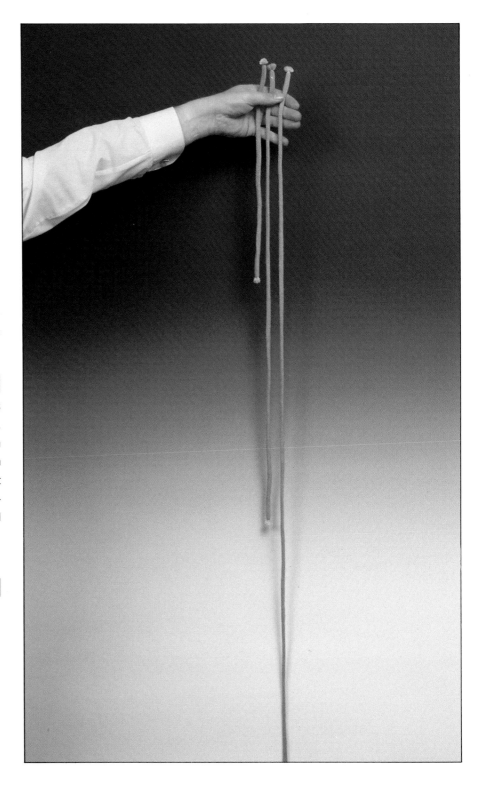

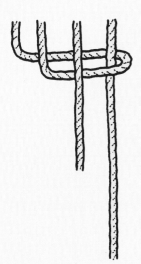

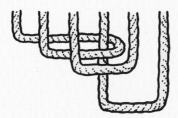

4 Bring the free end of the long length up and place it in the left hand to the right of the other lengths. Six ends are now held in the left hand.

2 Pass the right hand between the medium and the long lengths, take hold of the short length and bring it through, over the long length and then round the back of all the lengths so that the free end is brought into the left hand and held to the left of the other ends. Four ends are now held in the left hand.

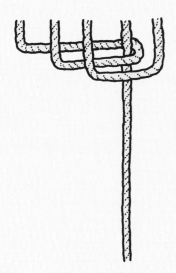

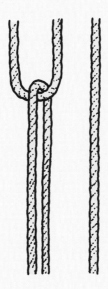

3 Bring the free end of the medium length up and place it in the left hand to the right of the other lengths. Five ends are now held in the left hand.

5 You are now ready to 'stretch' the ropes into equal lengths. With the right hand, take the three ends lying on the right; retain the three ends lying on the left in the left hand. Pull the ropes taut, all three pieces of rope actually appear to be the same length.

6 Drop the ends from the right hand and hold the ropes up in the left hand — the fingers of the left hand curling round and concealing the looped joins in the ropes.

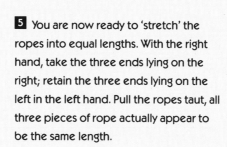

✩ COUNTING THE ROPES ✩

The lengths of rope can now be counted and shown separately. With the right hand, remove the one separate length (the original medium length) and display it, counting 'one'. Go to pick up a second length, secretly depositing the separate length and removing the two linked lengths, counting 'two'. Finally, pick up the separate length again and count 'three'. The audience believes they have seen three separate ropes, each of equal length.

✩ REVERSING THE EFFECT ✩

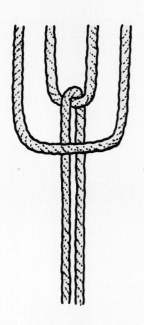

1 Bring the free end of the separate length and place it in the left hand to the left of the other ends.

2 Bring the left-hand portion of the long linked length up to the left.

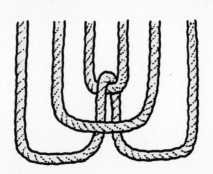

3 Bring the right hand portion up to the right.

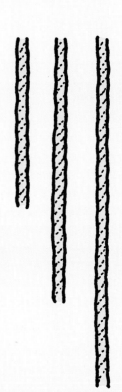

4 Take the first three ends on the right in the right hand, and simultaneously drop the remaining ends from the left hand and give the ropes a dramatic shake. They automatically separate to return to their original lengths: one short, one medium and one long.

THE WONDERFUL CHANGING BAG

· · · · ☆ ☆ ☆ · · · ·

The flat changing bag is a versatile property, which comes in handy for so many effects that it would be almost impossible for any magician to be without one.

Apparatus

The bag is made in two parts so that when assembled and finally made there are two separate compartments within it. You will require one piece of cloth approximately 50 × 20 cm (20 × 8 in) and one piece measuring 25 × 20 cm (10 × 8 in). The larger piece is folded in half, the smaller piece inserted between, and the edges are sewn together.

Working and Presentation

The bag can contain an item or items in one compartment so that when you wish to show that the bag is empty, the other compartment is turned inside out. The bag is turned back again and the items can be magically produced (from the other side). The bag can also appear to change one item for another. The empty side is first shown and a selected item is placed inside this compartment. A completely different item (already concealed) is then taken from the other compartment.

The item is shown and the now empty section of the bag can be displayed, proving there is nothing else left in the bag.

The magician can 'switch' one thing for another. For example, an empty box is placed in the bag, and then a duplicate box containing a ring is withdrawn.

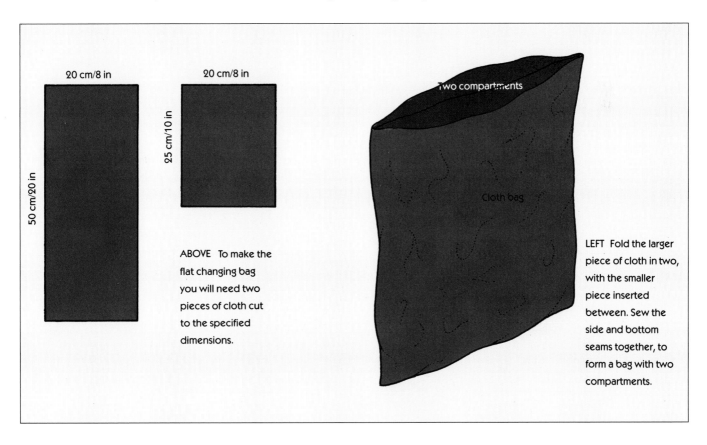

20 cm/8 in

20 cm/8 in

25 cm/10 in

50 cm/20 in

ABOVE To make the flat changing bag you will need two pieces of cloth cut to the specified dimensions.

Two compartments

Cloth bag

LEFT Fold the larger piece of cloth in two, with the smaller piece inserted between. Sew the side and bottom seams together, to form a bag with two compartments.

☆ 20 TRICKS USING THE ☆
WONDERFUL CHANGING BAG

If you have gone to the trouble of making up the bag, you will be looking for a number of effects to use it to its full advantage. Here are 20 miracles using the wonderful changing bag to get you started.

1 Several silk handkerchiefs are placed inside the empty bag, only to become knotted together.

2 Several silk handkerchiefs, together with a length of ribbon, are placed inside the bag. When they are withdrawn, the silks are seen to have tied themselves to the ribbon in a line.

3 Several silk handkerchiefs are placed inside the bag and made to disappear.

4 The bag is shown empty inside and out, yet when a spectator reaches inside, they bring out a quantity of silk handkerchiefs.

5 A pocket handkerchief is torn into pieces and becomes magically restored to its original shape and size.

6 A length of rope is cut into pieces and placed inside the bag only to become fully restored, the bag being shown completely empty once again.

7 A pack of shuffled cards is placed inside the bag. The performer names three cards, and miraculously pulls them out and displays them to the audience.

8 Petals are plucked from a rose and placed into the empty bag. The flower petals magically come together to form a perfect rose bloom.

9 Several knotted loops of rope magically link together in a chain.

10 A red silk handkerchief placed inside the bag magically changes to a yellow one.

11 A white handkerchief with dirty black stains on it becomes white and clean.

12 An item placed inside the bag replicates itself, so that another of the same mysteriously appears.

13 A piece of white paper of similar size to that of any paper currency is dropped inside the bag only to. reappear later as a perfectly printed note or bill.

14 When an object is placed, first in a small box, and then inside the bag, the object disappears. To do this, place an empty duplicate box into one compartment, and drop the full box into the other. When a spectator reaches inside and takes the planted box, it appears to be the original. When he or she opens the lid of the box, the item inside is no longer there.

15 Two loops of coloured ribbon are placed inside the bag and one further loop is placed inside the pocket. The pocket is shown empty (pocket dodge – ribbon loop pushed up to top of the pocket, lining brought out) and when taken out, the vanished ribbon is now seen tied between the other two.

16 The bag contains coins which display different dates. The magician makes a prediction on a piece of paper, stating the date of the coin which will be selected. A spectator places his hand into the bag and brings out one coin. Of course you have to make sure that all the coins on one side of the bag are of the same date.

17 How would you like to change an egg into a chicken without waiting as long as nature has allowed? Here is the best way – display an egg and drop it inside the bag. Strike a match and wave it below the bag. Smartly remove a toy chicken from the hidden compartment.

18 A blank piece of card magically produces a photo on one or both sides.

19 A spectator selects five letter cards from a lexicon pack and drops them inside the bag. Seconds later, when the cards are removed, it is seen that they spell M-A-G-I-C.

20 The last magical effect using the wonderful changing bag really is wonderful. It is a mentalist experiment using a sheet of newspaper, or a page torn from a periodical. The page is torn into pieces and these are dropped into the bag. The performer makes a prediction. He writes a few words on a slip of paper, and hands it to a spectator. Another spectator is requested to reach inside and bring out only one piece of paper. When the prediction is opened out and read aloud, the contents are the same as the words on the chosen scrap of newspaper.

In preparation for this experiment, tear the same sheets out of ten or twelve newspapers. They must all be the same in content. Then, holding these sheets together, tear off one small section of the sheets. These pieces are placed inside one compartment. Save a full sheet ready for tearing during performance. In front of the audience, tear the sheet into bits and drop them inside the empty side of the bag. When the selection is made, it is the opposite section of the bag that is offered to the spectator. This means that when his or her hand dips inside, whichever piece is brought out, the words are the same.

THE AMAZING CARD BOX

· · · · ☆ ☆ ☆ · · · ·

The card box is one of the most useful and versatile magic properties ever invented. As well as playing cards, slips of paper, photographs, paper currency etc can all be introduced into the working of the card box.

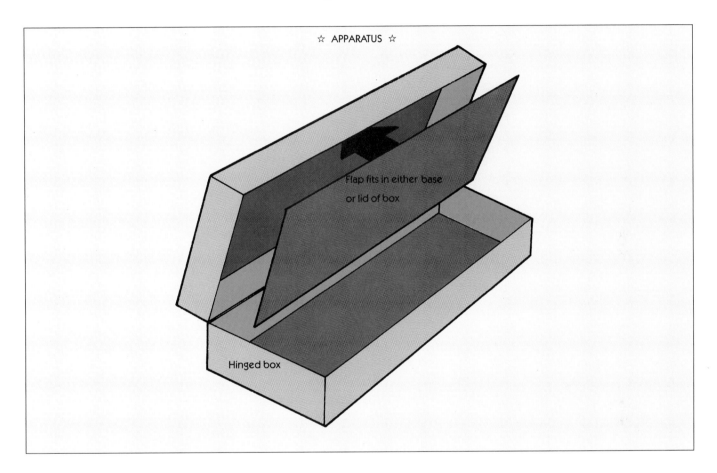

☆ APPARATUS ☆

Flap fits in either base or lid of box

Hinged box

Apparatus

It consists of a wooden box with a hinged lid. The lid and base have a recess into which a loose flap can be inserted. The flap is painted the same colour as the interior of the box. In most cases card boxes have black interiors.

Working and Presentation

Easy to work, the box is capable of making objects such as playing cards appear, disappear, change from one to another, change to something else entirely – it can even assist in performing a penetration.

☆ TO PRODUCE OBJECTS ☆

The object to be produced, say a card, is placed under the flap in the lid before the start of the performance. This means that the box can be shown to be completely empty inside. When the box is closed, the flap – and the card – falls to the base of the opposite side, and when it is opened once more, the card appears in position.

☆ TO CHANGE ONE CARD FOR ☆ ANOTHER

A different card to the one selected for display is secretly placed under the flap, before the start of the effect. The flap is positioned in the lid of the box. The box is shown empty; the second card is then displayed and placed inside. The box is closed. The box is reopened to show the magical transformation.

☆ TO VANISH CARDS ☆

The card box is empty at the start – the flap positioned in the lid. A card is dropped inside and the lid is closed. When it is reopened, the flap now covers the card, and so the box is shown to be empty – the card has apparently vanished.

☆ 20 TRICKS USING THE CARD BOX ☆

1 A playing card is shown, torn into pieces, and the pieces are dropped into the box. Moments later the card is seen to be completely restored.

2 The four twos magically change into the four aces.

3 A card chosen freely from a pack is dropped inside the box without the audience seeing its face. The magician predicts the name of the card before the experiment begins and reveals this to be the card inside the box.

4 A plain white card is placed inside the box, which is closed. The performer then opens the box and places a pencil inside it. When the box is opened a third time and the contents shown to the audience, the card is now seen to have ghostly writing on it.

5 The king and queen of hearts are placed inside the box. The jack of hearts is shown to the audience and placed inside the performer's trouser pocket. It vanishes (it is pushed up under the top lining of the trouser pocket) and when the box is reopened, the jack is with both king and queen.

6 A blank piece of paper placed inside the box magically changes into genuine paper currency.

7 A bank note placed inside the box changes into a larger denomination.

8 Unknown to the audience a card is stuck onto the outside base of the box using wax. With the flap in the upper section of the box, a duplicate card is dropped inside the box and the lid is closed. The box is tapped, the waxed card falls from the base onto the table and is shown to the audience.

The box is opened to show that the card has disappeared. This penetration effect will puzzle any audience.

9 Force onto a spectator the three of diamonds. Tell your audience that you will find the chosen card from the pack. Remove, say, the six of clubs, dropping it inside the empty box. Asking the spectator if that is the right card, he or she will obviously say 'no', but when the box is opened, written on the card are the words 'You will select the three of diamonds'. So you win in the end.

10 Two spectators each select a card from two different packs, without looking at them. These are placed inside the box. An envelope which has been on full view during the performance is opened and the contents read aloud. The prediction states that both spectators will select identical cards from the different packs, and these cards are named. This is simply a change of two cards for another two.

11 Numbers boldly marked onto pieces of white card, from one to six, are dropped into the box and the lid closed. A spectator is asked to freely select one. The performer can either predict beforehand or divine at the time what number has been selected. This is a simple switch of one set of genuine numbers from one to six for a set of six that are identical, for example, all fives.

12 Flat, coloured counters such as those used in board games are mixed up. They are placed inside the box. A spectator is asked to reach inside the box, without looking, and to remove one. The performer can always predict the colour chosen.

13 A piece of card is placed inside the box together with a postage stamp. The per-

former blows on the box. When the lid is opened the stamp is now seen to be stuck to the surface of the card ready to be mailed.

14 With a piece of white chalk, mark the name of a card, say, the four of spades, on one side of the flap. Put the four of spades from a pack of cards in the lid and cover with the flap – the marked side of the flap must face into the lid. A card is selected from a pack by a spectator, but not looked at. It is dropped inside the box and the lid is closed. Open the lid and drop inside a piece of white chalk, on top of the planted card. The spectator opens the box and finds the piece of chalk, the card, and sees that the card matches that of the chalked name mysteriously written on the bottom of the box (actually the flap).

15 A piece of white card is placed inside the box, it suddenly becomes a photograph of an object mentioned previously.

16 A crossword puzzle, ready to be solved, is placed inside the box and the lid closed. The box is opened and a pencil dropped in. When the box is reopened, the answers are all neatly marked in.

17 A card taken from the pack is marked with a bold X on its front. Placed inside the box, and reopened again, the card is seen now to have the X mark on its back.

18 Cards taken from a Lexicon pack are dropped inside the box, only to spell the word which the performer had previously predicted.

19 The performer magically prints his name on a blank business card and hands it out to a spectator.

20 Coloured gummed spots magically form a message on the surface of a blank card.

★ THE THUMB-TIP ★

If there is one small gadget that is more versatile than all the others put together, it is the thumb-tip. They come in all shapes and sizes, are made in different materials and are designed for a whole series of startling tricks which can be presented both in close-up and on stage.

A thumb-tip is not a magical gadget that can be easily made but it can be purchased cheaply. The magic dealer usually sells a selection of thumb-tips in plastic, rubber and metal. All are flesh-coloured (different shades are available), and all closely resemble a thumb, even to the nail markings.

The thumb-tip fits over the thumb, and can be used on either hand. In selecting a thumb-tip, the magician should obtain one which matches the size and flesh colour of his own thumb. The tip should be a comfortable fit, but it should be loose enough for it to come away from the thumb, and also to contain an item such as a small silk handkerchief. *During the routines that follow, the thumb-tip is very rarely seen.*

BELOW The thumb-tip – in which can be secreted a silk handkerchief, for example – should slip easily over the thumb.

BELOW The thumb-tip should match your own thumb in size and flesh colour. It should fit comfortably but not too tightly, otherwise it will be difficult to discard.

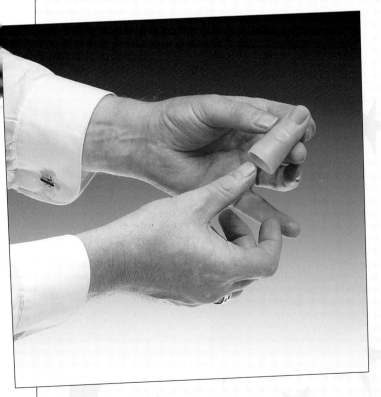

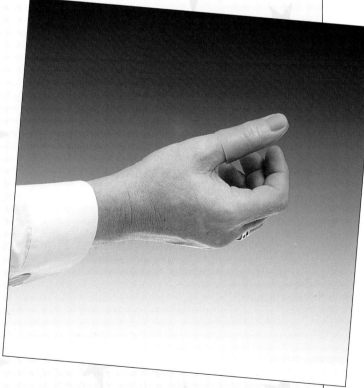

★ SHOWING THE HANDS EMPTY ★

With the thumb-tip on the right thumb (assuming that you are right-handed) you are ready to show your hands empty. The full length of the thumb-tip is never shown during display.

1 Point all fingers and thumbs towards the audience. Only the tips of the fingers and thumbs are on view, including the tip of the thumb-tip. This avoids the join between the end of the tip and the remainder of the genuine thumb being noticed.

2 If showing the hands in a static position, cross the thumb wearing the thumb-tip behind the opposite hand.

3 Again, from the audience's viewpoint, the presence of the thumb-tip is concealed.

★ OBTAINING THE THUMB-TIP ★ DURING PERFORMANCE

In many cases, the thumb-tip is not required until later in the routine, and so there is a correct procedure to secretly place it on the thumb. Depending on what particular effect you are planning, the thumb-tip is normally secreted inside a jacket pocket. On other occasions, where you intend going to a container or a section at the back of the table as part of the routine, secretly pick it up from there. Should it be used in an opening effect, it can of course be worn on the thumb at your entrance.

★ EFFECTS USING THE ★ THUMB-TIP

PRODUCING A HANDKERCHIEF FROM THIN AIR

· · · · ☆ ☆ ☆ · · · ·

Effect

The magician shows both hands to be empty. Making a catching motion in the air, the performer forms his right hand into a clenched fist. From the fist is magically extracted a coloured silk handkerchief.

Apparatus

A thumb-tip and a small silk handkerchief.

Set-up

Secrete the handkerchief into the thumb-tip prior to the start of the effect, making sure one corner is towards the open end of the thumb-tip for easy extraction. The thumb-tip should be worn on the thumb.

Working and Presentation

To pleasing patter lines, show the hands to be empty in the manner previously described. Fingers and thumbs are wiggled, hands always on the move. With the right hand, reach into the air making a catching motion. In doing so, allow the thumb to bend inwards so that it is towards the palm of the hand, the fingers also coming inwards to form a fist. Withdraw the thumb. The thumb-tip is now firmly contained within the first with its open mouth towards the top. With the first finger and thumb of the left hand, pull out the silk from the tip. From the

audience's viewpoint you appear to be extracting the silk from the fist itself.

There are two possible ways of discarding the thumb-tip after use. The first method is to allow the thumb to re-enter the tip so that it is back in its original position. The second method is executed when the silk is being displayed after its production. As the silk is discarded or pocketed, the thumb-tip secretly goes with it. This latter method is better than the first since your hands are genuinely empty, ready for the continuance of other effects which do not require the gadget.

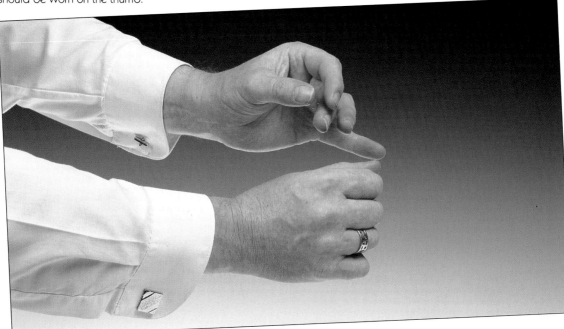

LEFT The thumb-tip has been secretly removed from the right thumb to be clutched, hidden, in the fist.

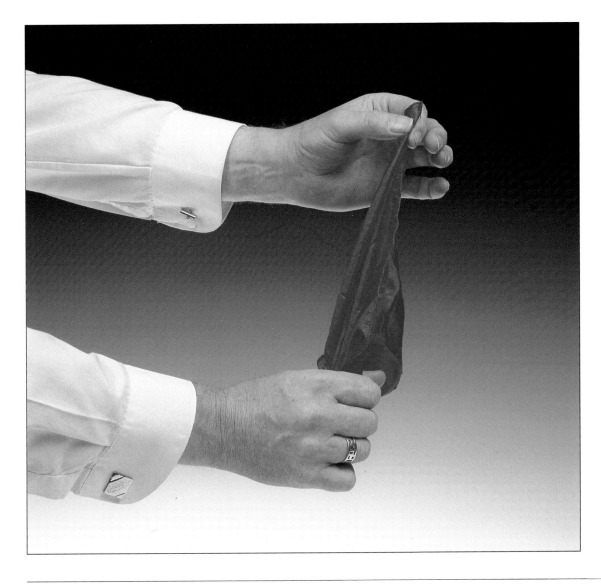

LEFT Now the silk handkerchief can be magically drawn from the fist.

VANISHING A SILK HANDKERCHIEF
· · · · ☆ ☆ ☆ · · · ·

Vanishing a handkerchief is as simple as producing it. The empty thumb-tip is already on the thumb at the start, or can be secretly obtained from the pocket.

Apparatus

A thumb-tip and a small silk handkerchief.

Working and Presentation

Show both hands to be empty and curl in the fingers and thumb of the right hand so as to make a fist. With the thumb-tip now removed from the thumb and held in the clenched fist, tuck the silk into the hidden thumb-tip.

Once the silk is inside, it is an easy matter to insert the thumb back into the tip so that both hands can then be opened to show that the silk has completely vanished.

VANISHING A LIGHTED CIGARETTE

· · · · · ☆ ☆ ☆ · · · ·

A popular effect among close-up workers, the vanish of a lighted cigarette in a borrowed pocket handkerchief always seems to amaze and amuse onlookers.

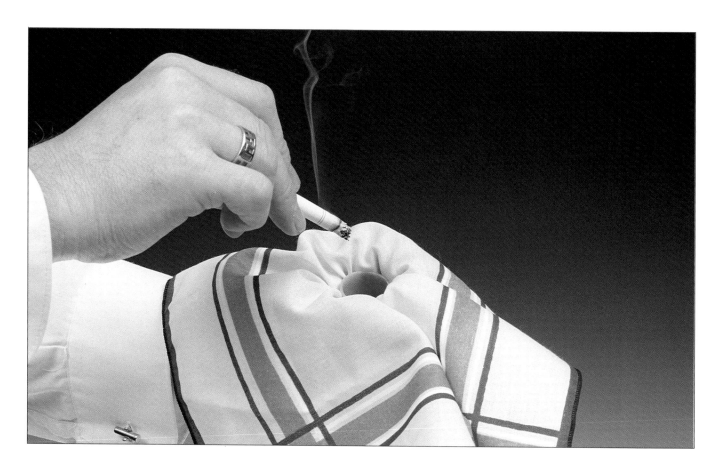

ABOVE The lighted cigarette is actually dropped into the thumb-tip and not into the 'well' made in the handkerchief as it appears to the audience.

Effect

A pocket handkerchief is borrowed from a member of the audience, thus proving that it is genuine and is of value to that particular person. The handkerchief is draped over the left hand which forms a fist. A lighted cigarette, which can be borrowed, or belong to the performer, is dropped into the central folds of the borrowed handkerchief. As the performer patters he is quite unaware of the smoke which is seen rising from inside the handkerchief. The audience laughs, and as the performer becomes aware there is something wrong, he notices the handker-chief is on fire. Stubbing out the lighted cigarette within the material of the handker-chief, the performer allows this to drop open showing that it is quite unharmed. The handkerchief is returned to its rightful owner.

Apparatus

A thumb-tip; a half-smoked cigarette and a box of matches, just in case a cigarette can-not be borrowed.

Set-up

The thumb-tip is already on the thumb prior to the start of the trick.

Working and Presentation

During this effect the hands are never really shown to be empty, since you are not intending to produce something from them. Hold the hands naturally, and bend the thumb – wearing the tip – inwards so that it is not in full view.

Borrow a pocket handkerchief from a spectator, displaying it on both sides, to show its quality and the fact that it is intact. Drape the handkerchief over the left fist. Use the thumb wearing the tip to make a well for the cigarette to be dropped inside. Dip the thumb in several times, making an indentation. Pull the thumb away leaving the tip behind concealed in the handkerchief. Simply drop the cigarette, lighted end downwards, into the thumb-tip so that a stream of smoke rises for the audience to see. The audience's laughter draws your attention to the 'burning' handkerchief; repeatedly stub out the cigarette with the thumb and secretly withdraw the tip on the thumb the final time. Display the handkerchief face on to the audience, keeping both thumbs behind the top corners of the handkerchief which can be displayed for some length of time so that the audience realizes that it is intact. Return the borrowed handkerchief to the spectator, and should you wish to discard the thumb-tip at this stage, it can be ditched when the matchbox is replaced inside a pocket.

BELOW The cigarette can then be safely stubbed out against the base of the thumb-tip.

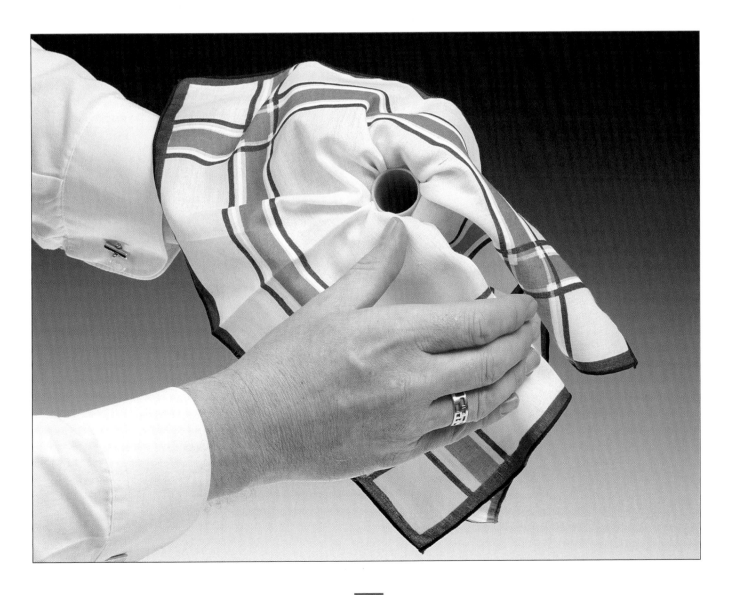

CHILDREN WILL NEED SUPERVISION

BURNT AND RESTORED HANDKERCHIEF
· · · · ☆ ☆ ☆ · · · ·

This is yet another experiment using a burnt and restored theme,
as well as making use of the faithful thumb-tip.

BELOW In the set-up, a specially prepared portion of cloth is inserted into the thumb-tip.

Effect

The performer borrows a pocket handkerchief from a member of the audience. The centre of the handkerchief is found and pushed up through the fingers and thumb of the left hand. The flame from a cigarette lighter burns the centre of the handkerchief. Meanwhile, the performer has been explaining that it is possible to burn flammable material without harming it. Seeing that this may not be the case in this experiment, the performer stubs out the flames, flicks out the handkerchief, displays it to show it is restored, and returns it to the owner undamaged.

Apparatus

A thumb-tip, a cigarette lighter and a small piece of white cotton material taken from a pocket handkerchief. Gather up the four corners of this piece of cloth and either sew them together or bind them up with a small length of clear adhesive tape.

Set-up

Secrete the prepared piece of cloth, with the taped ends downwards, within the thumb-tip. Place the prepared thumb-tip in your right jacket pocket next to the cigarette lighter.

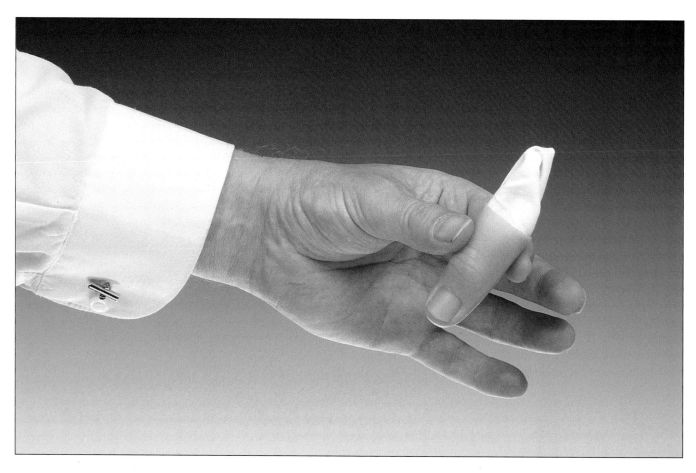

Working and Presentation

At the start of the experiment request the loan of a man's white pocket handkerchief. It is important that at least the middle part of the handkerchief is white so that it matches the cloth secreted in the thumb-tip.

Drape the pocket handkerchief over the left fist. Put the right hand in the right jacket pocket to remove the cigarette lighter, and at the same time push the thumb into the thumb-tip. Remove both thumb-tip and lighter from the pocket. Explain that you plan to demonstrate just how some materials burn and some do not. Place the lighter onto the table and make a well in the centre of the handkerchief with the thumb (and the tip), leaving the tip behind. Casually show that the right hand is empty as you proceed to pull up what appears to be the central portion of the handkerchief – in fact it is the portion of cloth concealed in the thumb-tip that comes into view. This is the portion which is set alight. Operate the cigarette lighter and wave the flame quickly over the edges of the handkerchief to show that it is 'inflammable'. Now bring the flame to the cloth concealed within the tip, and wave it over the fabric until it catches light. Pretend not to see this at first, then feign alarm and stub out the flames with the thumb – the cloth inside the thumb-tip is by now little more than ashes. Before withdrawing the thumb for the last time, slip on the thumb-tip. Remove the lighter from the table, put it into the right jacket pocket and discard the thumb-tip at the same time. The right hand comes out of the pocket clean and empty.

Looking at what appears to be a burnt handkerchief, make a magical pass over it, then open the handkerchief out to show that it is now fully restored. Return the borrowed handkerchief to the spectator.

Note: when practising this effect, it is always sensible to have an ashtray nearby since burning cloth can accidentally float away as it disintegrates.

LEFT & BELOW It is the cloth secreted in the thumb-tip which is set alight. From the audience's viewpoint, however, it looks like part of the genuine handkerchief.

PASSING THE SALT

· · · · ☆ ☆ ☆ · · · ·

For many years magicians have been making salt travel from one clenched fist to the other, relying upon the thumb-tip as the perfect aid. The salt transformation effect seems impossible since the performer is dealing with small grains of salt which are unlike other props such as handkerchiefs or cigarettes.

Effect

Both the performer's hands are shown empty. From a salt shaker, salt is poured into the performer's left first, his right fist being shown empty.

The performer blows towards the left fist, and, upon opening each finger, every grain of salt is seen to have vanished. Performing a catching motion with the right hand, this is instantly made into a fist and from it is poured the vanished salt.

Apparatus

A thumb-tip; a salt shaker (the type with a screw-on top is best for this purpose) containing salt; a glass bowl or ashtray.

Set-up

Put the salt shaker at the back of your table, behind other properties, together with the thumb-tip which should also be out of view.

Working and Presentation

Show that both hands are absolutely empty – the thumb-tip is not being worn at this stage. Pick up the salt shaker with the right hand, at the same time secretly inserting the thumb into the thumb-tip. Place the shaker on the front of the table. Use the right hand to bend the fingers of the left hand into a fist, loading the thumb-tip, with its open mouth upward, into the fist.

Remove the lid of the salt shaker and pour the contents into the fist (thumb-tip). It is important to leave space for the insertion of the thumb. Allow some grains of salt to pour down the fingers and push the right thumb down inside the clenched left fist as if salt is starting to overflow at the top. In doing so, push the thumb into the tip, extract both thumb and tip, quickly showing that the right hand is empty, and then form a fist with the right hand. Now for the transformation. Open the left hand, stretching each finger out to show that the salt has vanished. Invert the right hand over the top of the clear bowl or ashtray so that the salt within the concealed thumb-tip pours from the fist. Secretly transfer the thumb-tip onto the thumb.

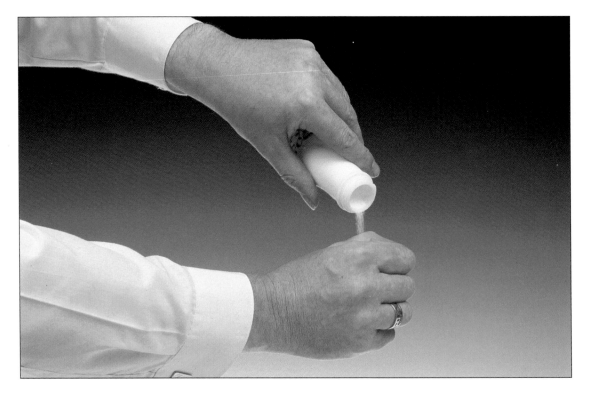

LEFT The salt is tipped into the performer's fist. It is, in fact, being tipped into the concealed thumb-tip.

THE PENETRATING THUMB

· · · · ☆ ☆ ☆ · · · ·

Matter through matter — here is a trick that will make your
audiences gasp.

Effect

The performer pushes his thumb right through the centre of a borrowed pocket handkerchief. Both the performer's thumb and the spectator's pocket handkerchief can be thoroughly examined.

Apparatus

A thumb-tip.

Set-up

Wear the thumb-tip on the right thumb.

Working and Presentation

Borrow a handkerchief from a member of the audience. Then explain and demonstrate the actions of the trick: that you will drape the handkerchief over the clenched fist and that you will push your thumb right through the centre of the handkerchief. Demonstrate this action by pushing the right thumb (wearing the tip) into the well of the fist. Withdraw the thumb leaving the thumb-tip concealed in the left fist. Now actually drape the handkerchief over the top of the left fist and use the right thumb to form a well in the centre of the handkerchief. Push the thumb itself and the central material of the handkerchief into the thumb-tip. Then remove the left hand to show that the 'thumb' has penetrated the handkerchief — the thumb-tip on top traps the material of the handkerchief while the genuine thumb fits comfortably within the mould of the tip.

To reverse the procedure, grip the handkerchief and the thumb-tip with the left hand and pull both away. Pocket them and bring the audience's attention towards the right thumb. Remove the handkerchief from the pocket, display it and hand it back to its owner.

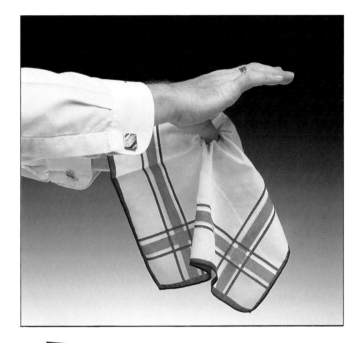

LEFT In making a well in the handkerchief, the right thumb is pushed onto the thumb-tip already concealed in the left fist.

BELOW When the right hand is held up, the 'thumb' appears to have penetrated the handkerchief.

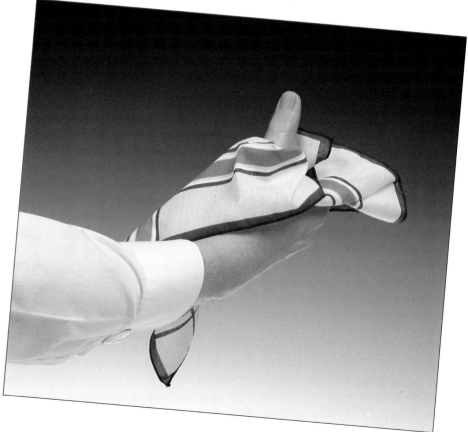

MAGIC IN CLOSE-UP

The most popular branch of magic, close-up magic, is ideal for the semi-professional or amateur who likes to entertain, impromptu, at parties, or any social gathering. Close-up magic makes use of almost every small household object you can think of, from matches to safety-pins, to coins, keys and knives.

The special qualities that make a good close-up magician are the nerve to perform on the spur of the moment, and the ability to select the most suitable members of the audience for specific tricks. The close-up performer should always pay special attention to his or her personal hygiene. The hands are always the centre of attention, and so nails should be clean and trimmed and shirt sleeves should be crisp and stiff.

Because of the proximity of the audience in close-up magic, it is often recommended that the magician uses a mouthwash!

A DATE WITH A MAGICIAN

The famous Okito box, made in solid brass, silver or plastic, is still very popular with close-up performers. However, most seem to use the box in the way it was first originated, adding no ingenuity or flair. I hope to have added something that little bit extra in this particular version.

Effect

The performer displays a small pillbox, of any material. A coin is borrowed from a member of the audience and is placed inside the box itself, while the performer turns away so as not to see the transaction. The cap is placed on the box.

Immediately, the performer, numeral by numeral, announces the date of the borrowed coin. The spectator who loaned the coin verifies that the predicted date is correct.

The performer continues the effect by placing the sealed box on top of his or her clenched left fist. He taps the box. The coin magically penetrates through the material of the box, through the hand and falls on top of the table. The box is shown and handed out for examination. The coin is then returned to its lender.

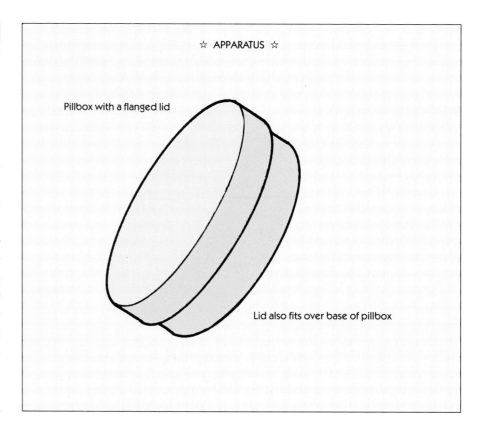

☆ APPARATUS ☆

Pillbox with a flanged lid

Lid also fits over base of pillbox

Apparatus

A pillbox or a container with a push-on (*not* a screw-on) lid. It is important that the lid can also fit over the *base* of the box.

Working and Presentation

First ask for the loan of a coin, any coin which can fit inside the box. Once a spectator has provided a coin, turn away. Still holding the box towards the audience, ask the spectator to drop the coin, date-side up, inside. Then ask the spectator to place the cap or lid on the box. Now hold the box, sealed with the cap, in the right hand. Rattle the box with the coin inside to prove that it is still there at this stage.

Holding the box in the cupped right hand remove the lid with the left hand to show that the coin is still there. The performer turns away to make sure the audience are aware that at no time do you actually look at the coin. In replacing the cap onto the box, execute a very clever, yet simple move. Pivot over the box with the right hand so that its base is now upwards, the coin still inside, but resting on the palm. With the left hand, immediately place the lid of the box on top of the *base*. Shake the box, gripped with the right-hand fingers and the thumb, even in this position the coin is heard to rattle inside. Tilting the box towards the audience, secretly glance at the date of the coin which is now exposed underneath. Now you can divine the date of the borrowed coin.

The second part of the effect is almost ready for presentation. With the box, containing the coin, resting on the palm of the right hand, remove the box with the left hand, and at the same time pivot over the right hand to palm the coin. Place the box on top of the clenched fist of the right hand, which is secretly concealing the coin. Simply tap the box with the left hand and allow the coin to fall onto the table from within. That is the penetration. Pick the box up in the left hand and throw it down onto the table. The lid and base will separate and both parts can be examined.

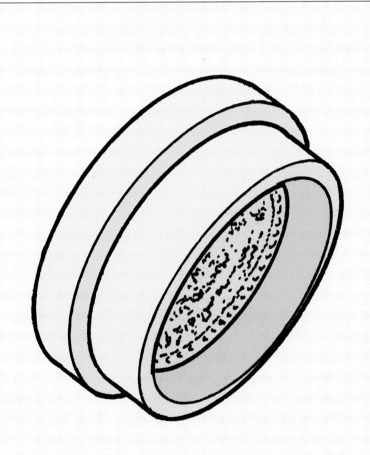

LEFT With the lid placed on the *base* of the pillbox, the box can be tilted forwards slightly to allow the performer to glance the date of the coin.

SPENT MATCHES

· · · · · ☆ ☆ ☆ · · · ·

For this quick trick all you will need is an empty matchbox, four live matchsticks and three spent ones.

Effect

The performer empties out the contents of a matchbox to reveal that there are only four matches left. Dropping three of these inside the box and closing the tray, the performer strikes the fourth match and waves it around the box in a mysterious fashion.

When the box is opened and the contents tipped out, the matchsticks are now found to be spent ones. The box is otherwise shown to be empty.

Apparatus and Set-up

Prepare the box as illustrated, cutting a section away from one end of the inner tray. In setting the trick, wedge the three unseen spent matchsticks between the inner tray and outer sleeve. Keep the box open at this position. Drop the four live matchsticks into the tray.

Working and Presentation

Display the opened box and tip out the four matchsticks onto the table. Show that the inside of the box is empty. Drop three of the matchsticks back inside, and put the fourth in a pocket. Hold the box in the left hand and tilt it so that the three live matchsticks secretly slide out through the slot and into your awaiting hand. Close the matchbox allowing the spent matchsticks, which are wedged at the top, to automatically fall inside the tray. With the left hand, go to the pocket as if to withdraw the fourth live match, but in doing so drop two of the three matchsticks already palmed, bringing out only one. Strike the live match against the matchbox and wave it around the box. Open the box and empty the contents onto the table to reveal three *spent* matchsticks.

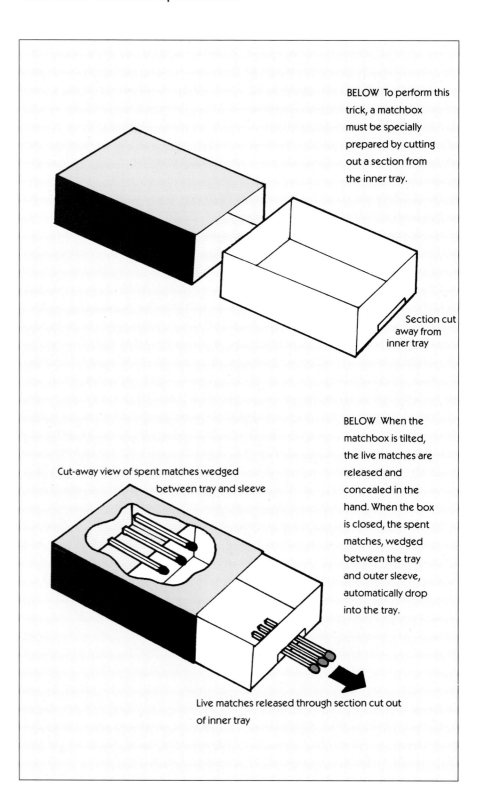

BELOW To perform this trick, a matchbox must be specially prepared by cutting out a section from the inner tray.

Section cut away from inner tray

BELOW When the matchbox is tilted, the live matches are released and concealed in the hand. When the box is closed, the spent matches, wedged between the tray and outer sleeve, automatically drop into the tray.

Cut-away view of spent matches wedged between tray and sleeve

Live matches released through section cut out of inner tray

DOMINO CARD
· · · · ☆ ☆ ☆ · · · ·

Although there is a certain amount of mentalism connected with this next effect, it is really a close-up trick, and one which baffles the onlookers.

Effect

A spectator is requested to take a pack of cards and then to freely select 12 cards; these should be laid out on view, face-up.

A set of dominoes is spread out on the table with the spotted sides uppermost. A second spectator is requested to complete a one-player version of dominoes, matching each domino until two numbers, one at each end, result. The spectator calls out the two numbers and the total. The first spectator is then requested to count out the same number along the line of cards and then to pull away the card at that position. Inside a sealed envelope is the prediction, which, when read aloud reveals not only the two domino numbers but the suit and value of the card.

Apparatus

A pack of cards (if you borrow these from a spectator the effect would be enhanced); a set of dominoes; an envelope; a piece of paper or card, and a pencil or pen.

Set-up

Beforehand, remove one of the dominoes from the set, say, one with three spots on one side and two on the other. These numbers are the numbers that will appear at the ends of the chain when the domino game is completed. In this way you will know the totalled number (in this case 5), and the position of the card to be divined.

Working and Presentation

Display the pack of cards and shuffle them. Immediately hand the cards to a member of the audience. Then ask the spectator to select 12 cards from the pack and display them, face-up, in a line. Take note of the name of the card situated at position five.

Produce the set of dominoes and scatter them on the top of the table, with the spots uppermost. Ask a second spectator to assist by playing the game of dominoes alone, matching each domino, until she is left with two unmatching dominoes, one at each end of the chain. Because a three- and two-spot domino has been removed from the set, the end numbers are three and two. While the domino game is being played, take the card, write on it the prediction of the two end numbers and the name of the playing card at that position. Seal the prediction into an envelope and hand it to another spectator for safe-keeping.

As soon as the spectator has completed the domino game, ask her to add both end spots together and announce the total. Now ask the spectator in charge of the 12 playing cards to name aloud the card at the fifth position. Remove the prediction slip from the envelope, then read aloud its contents. The numbers at each end of the chain of dominoes are correct, and the name of the card, one from 12 which were freely taken from a pack of 52 by a spectator, is correct as well!

CHILDREN WILL NEED SUPERVISION

M A T C H - I C

· · · · · ☆ ☆ ☆ · · · ·

A simple book of matches is used for this close-up effect.

Effect

The performer displays a book of matches, showing that the contents consist of all live matches. Removing one match from the book, it is struck against the striking surface, then waved around the book. When the matches are shown again, one match among the others is seen to be spent.

Apparatus

A book of matches.

Set-up

Bend one match away from its original position, strike its head and blow out the flame. Have the book of matches inside your right jacket pocket.

Working and Presentation

With your right hand, remove the book of matches from your pocket, holding the base between the finger and thumb so that the spent match, which is still attached to the book, is hidden, as illustrated. Now, with your left hand, remove one of the live matches and strike it against the book of matches. Close the packet from front to back, pivoting the bent match so that it is now inside the book; secure the cover. Wave the lighted match around the packet, and then open the cover to show that one match magically appears spent.

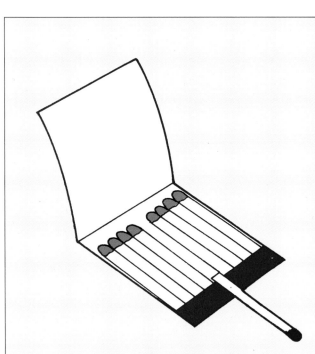

ABOVE To set-up this trick, one match from a book of matches is bent downwards. The head is struck and blown out. The book of matches is put inside the right jacket pocket.

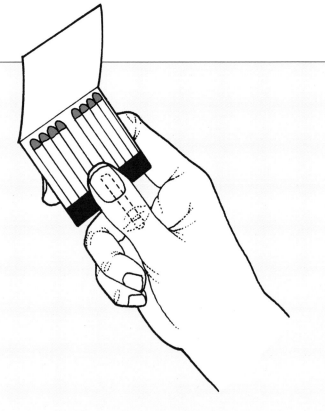

ABOVE When performing this close-up effect, the spent match is concealed by the thumb.

ODDS OR EVENS

· · · · · ☆ ☆ ☆ · · · ·

The perfect puzzler to perform any time, close-up and surrounded.

Effect

The magician displays a matchbox, which he rests on the table so that it is in full view during the experiment. He tells a spectator that he can always prove him or her wrong and will even place a bet on the teaser. He further states that the box is filled with an odd or even number of matches and that whichever choice the spectator makes – odd or even – will be proved, by the performer, to be wrong. The spectator announces whichever he wishes, odd or even. The inside tray of the matchbox is slid open and the matches tipped out. If the spectator had selected even, the matches when counted total an odd number, and should he decide upon odd, the matches

amount to an even number. This sequence can be repeated.

Apparatus

An ordinary matchbox, and just nineteen matchsticks.

Set-up

Prepare the box beforehand. Place six matches inside the box, then place a seventh diagonally across the others, thus wedging the first six matches inside the box. You will find that by inverting the tray all seven matches will retain their position and will not fall out. On top of these matches place another twelve and slide the tray into its outer cover. You are all set to begin.

Working and Presentation

The secret to this puzzling effect is extremely simple whatever choice the spectator makes. If the spectator selects even, slide out the inner tray showing the matches inside, turn the tray upside down and allow the matches to fall out. Only the twelve matches on top of the wedged ones actually leave the tray to fall onto the table. Pocket the tray and count the matches – an even number results.

If, on the other hand, the spectator selects odd, simply exert pressure on the sides of the tray to dislodge the wedged match.

Then turn the tray upside down allowing all nineteen matches to fall out to produce the required odd number.

LEFT To set-up this effect, six matchsticks are dropped into the empty tray; a seventh is then placed diagonally on top. The first six matches are now effectively wedged and will not fall out when the tray is turned upside down. A further twelve matches are dropped on top and the tray is slid into its outer sleeve.

ONE IN THE MIDDLE

· · · · ☆ ☆ ☆ · · · ·

This baffling close-up effect can be presented impromptu,
anywhere and under any conditions.

Effect

Five cards are shown, two identical pairs
and one single. The row of cards is stuck
together with the pairs positioned at each
end and the odd card in the middle. After
reversing the row, so that the backs of the
cards are now in view, the performer hands
a spectator a paper-clip, asking him or her
to clip the odd card. It all looks so easy, yet
when the cards are reversed again, it is seen
that the wrong card has been clipped.

Apparatus

Two pairs of identical cards taken from two
packs of cards, and one odd card from one
of the packs.

Set-up

Arrange the cards in a row, from left to right,
starting with the first pair, sticking each card
on top of the next, covering about two-thirds
of the face. The central card is the odd one,
followed by the second pair. Once stuck
together, the unit can be handled as one,
but referred to as a row of cards.

Working and Presentation

The effect requires no skill or dexterity at all.
Try it for yourself and you will find that although the central card viewed from the
picture side appears to be the odd card,
when the row is reversed, and the clip is
placed onto what appears to be the central
card, it is not. When the row is shown again,
face-up, the clip is always attached to the
front card of the five. The spectator never
manages to locate the middle card.

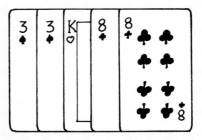

1 To set up this trick, stick together a
row of cards, face-up, in the following
order: one identical pair, one odd card –
the king of hearts, for example – and a
second identical pair.

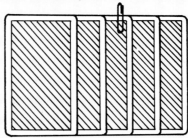

2 Reverse the prepared row of cards
and ask a spectator to clip the king of
hearts. The paper clip shows his obvious
choice.

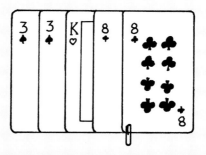

3 Reverse the row of cards so that they
are again face-up to reveal the clipped
card. The spectator has, in fact, clipped
the front card and not the king of hearts
at all.

KEY-RIFFIC!

· · · · ☆ ☆ ☆ · · · ·

This is a close-up effect using a key on a key-ring.

Effect

The performer displays a key secured to a key-ring. The key is removed and handed to a spectator who assists in making it vanish from within a pocket handkerchief. The key then reappears on the key-ring again.

Apparatus

Three identical keys. A key-ring which snaps open and shut. Two pocket handkerchiefs – one genuine and the other faked (see the Set-up below).

Set-up

Sew one of the keys into the hem of one of the handkerchiefs. Secure the two remaining keys onto the key-ring and place this unit in the right jacket pocket together with the faked handkerchief. Place the real handkerchief in the left jacket pocket.

Working and Presentation

Remove the key-ring from the right jacket pocket with the first two fingers and the thumb gripping one of the keys to hide it from view. To the audience, the key-ring appears to have only one key on it.

Ask a spectator to open the key-ring and remove the visible key and hold it for you. With the left hand, remove the real handkerchief from the left jacket pocket. Place the key-ring, with the second key still hidden, on the handkerchief and gather up the four corners to form a bag. Hand this to a second member of the audience to hold by the gathered corners.

With the right hand, remove the second – faked – handkerchief from the right jacket pocket. Take the key from the first spectator and pretend to place it underneath the handkerchief and up into the left hand. In reality, palm the key in the right hand and at the same time grip the key sewn into the fake handkerchief with the left hand. It is this key which you invite a spectator to feel through the fabric of the handkerchief. Secretly pocket the palmed loose key later.

Now for the transformation. Take hold of one corner of the handkerchief, and suddenly reveal that the key has vanished. Show the handkerchief all round. Ask the second assisting spectator to unwrap the handkerchief 'bag' to reveal that the 'vanished' key is now secured to the key-ring.

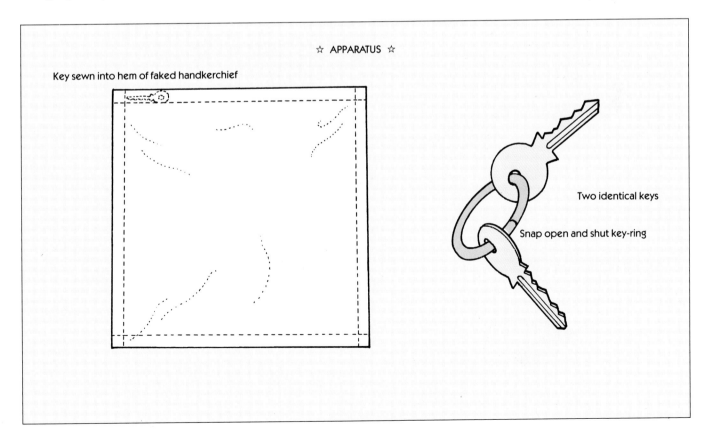

☆ APPARATUS ☆

Key sewn into hem of faked handkerchief

Two identical keys

Snap open and shut key-ring

MISCELLANEOUS MAGIC

Under this heading comes magic using all types of articles, effects which are not necessarily categorized as a particular branch of magic. Some new and original concepts have been included, tricks which have never before appeared in print.

Miscellaneous magic covers platform, close-up and impromptu work, providing something for all.

FAN-TASTIC!

· · · · · ☆ ☆ ☆ · · · · ·

This card trick is as effective on the stage as it is in close-up.

Effect

From a pack of cards, three cards are selected by three different spectators. An electric fan which has been on full power during the performance on a nearby table, looks normal, but when it is unplugged it slowly and mysteriously reveals the cards, one on each of the revolving blades.

Apparatus

A strong electric fan. Three miniature, patience-size cards of your choice – these are the cards which will be revealed on the blades of the fan. A pack of cards.

Set-up

Stick the three patience cards to the blades of the fan, faces outwards of course. You will find that when the fan is on full power the cards are not recognizable – only a splurge of colour seems to whizz around and around. That is the secret of this effect.

Working and Presentation

Do not draw attention to the fan until you have forced the correct cards onto three members of the audience. (See Chapter 2 for various ways of forcing cards.) Ensure that the names of the cards are announced. Then introduce the fan into the performance; unplug it, and as the fan slows down, the correct cards make their appearance.

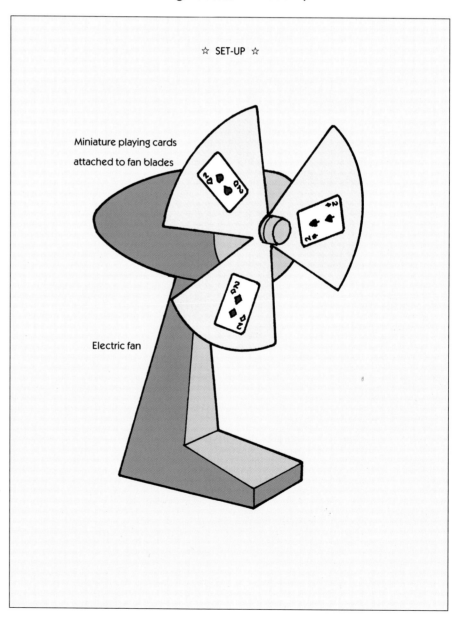

☆ SET-UP ☆

Miniature playing cards attached to fan blades

Electric fan

STIFF'N ROPE

• • • • ☆ ☆ ☆ • • • •

A touch of magic from India, this platform item resembles the theme of the Indian Rope Trick.

Effect

A length of rope is balanced on the end of the first finger, and magically becomes rigid. It then assumes its original limp form after the trick has been accomplished.

Apparatus

A length of soft white rope.

Set-up

Sew a small loop of flesh-coloured cotton thread to one end of the rope.

Working and Presentation

With the right hand, hold the end of the rope, concealing the loop of thread. To balance the end of the rope on the left first finger, slip this finger into the loop and with the right hand, hold the opposite end of the rope upwards. The rope becomes stiff and rigid. Pull the hands against each other to ensure that the rope is kept taut.

To complete the trick, disengage the finger from the loop and the length of rope resumes its original form.

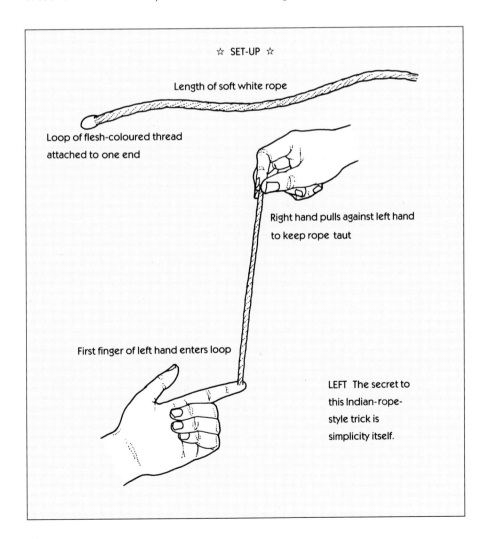

☆ SET-UP ☆

Length of soft white rope

Loop of flesh-coloured thread attached to one end

Right hand pulls against left hand to keep rope taut

First finger of left hand enters loop

LEFT The secret to this Indian-rope-style trick is simplicity itself.

CURRENCY-CUT

· · · · · ☆ ☆ ☆ · · · · ·

Effect

A borrowed bank note is slid inside a flat tube of paper. The audience clearly sees the paper currency through the two windows cut out at each end. The tube and bank note are cut in half with a pair of scissors, yet moments later the note is pulled from the wreckage, undamaged and apparently restored.

Apparatus

A paper tube made from a long narrow envelope. Seal the envelope, then cut a strip off each end to form a tube. Now cut two slits in the rear of the tube about 5 cm (2 in) apart, they must be long enough to allow the bank note to slide through them. Cut out two square window shapes from the front of the flat tube.

Set-up

Have the paper tube nearby, with the slit side facing downwards, together with a pair of scissors.

Working and Presentation

Borrow a bank note and slide it through the paper tube so that it comes out the opposite end. Push it back inside again, this time forcing it out through one slit and back into the tube through the other slit, so that the central portion of the bank note is outside the paper tube. The audience can clearly see the note through the cut-out windows in the front face of the tube.

Cut through the centre of the tube, but slide the scissors behind the note, so that you only cut the tube. Hold together both cut sections as you quickly pull out the five pound note and show it to be restored. Crumple or cut up the paper tube to destroy the evidence.

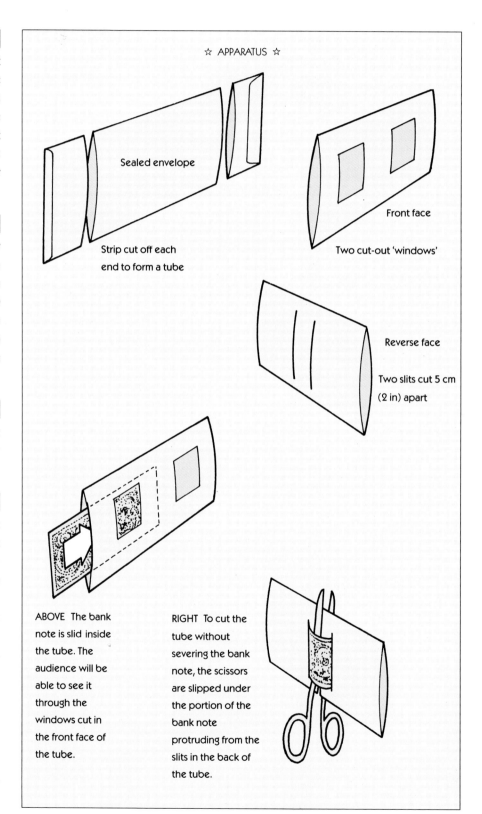

☆ APPARATUS ☆

Sealed envelope

Strip cut off each end to form a tube

Front face

Two cut-out 'windows'

Reverse face

Two slits cut 5 cm (2 in) apart

ABOVE The bank note is slid inside the tube. The audience will be able to see it through the windows cut in the front face of the tube.

RIGHT To cut the tube without severing the bank note, the scissors are slipped under the portion of the bank note protruding from the slits in the back of the tube.

DYE-A-BOLICAL
· · · · ☆ ☆ ☆ · · · ·

Magicians have been using the Okito tumbler for many years. It consists of a transparent plastic tumbler which has a central hollow tube down its centre. The outside surface of the tumbler is fluted or marked, so the inner tube is invisible at a distance. Items such as a silk handkerchief – can be secreted within the central hollow tube, and pulled out of the tumbler, filled with liquid, quite dry.

Effect

The magician displays a clear tumbler in his left hand. Lifting a clear jug of water in his right hand, he commences to pour some into a tumbler. The water mysteriously turns red. From the centre of the tumbler the performer produces a bright red, perfectly dry, silk handkerchief.

Apparatus

An Okito tumbler, a 30 cm (12 in) square silk handkerchief, red dye (cochineal), and a jug of water.

Set-up

Before the performance, pour some red dye into the main part of the Okito tumber – *not* into the hollow tube. Place the red silk hand-kerchief inside the hollow tube, tucking it down with a pencil so that it lies well down in the base of the unit. It should be tucked well down so that the cupped left hand, holding the tumbler, can hide the silk hand-kerchief from view.

Working and Presentation

Display the tumbler by picking it up with the left hand, fingers cupped around it so that the silk hidden inside the hollow tube is concealed. With the right hand, lift up the jug of water and pour the liquid into the main part of the tumbler. The water turns red as it is mixed with the dye. With the aid of a pair of tweezers, produce the red silk hand-kerchief from the centre of the tumbler, and show that it is quite dry.

LEFT The Okito tumbler is made of clear plastic, and has a hollow tube down the centre.

RIGHT The fluted walls of the tumbler conceal the hollow tube from the audience.

RIGHT Even with the Okito tumbler filled with liquid, a silk handkerchief can be drawn out of the inner hollow tube and shown to be quite dry.

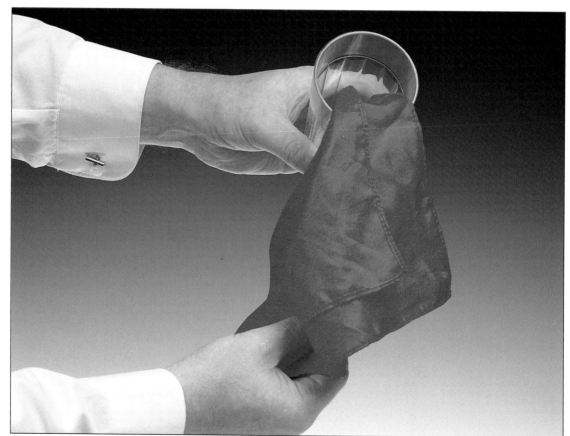

CHILDREN WILL NEED SUPERVISION

BAFFLING BEAKER

· · · · · ☆ ☆ ☆ · · · ·

Here is one piece of magical apparatus which can conjure up literally hundreds of tricks.

Effect

The Baffling Beaker appears to be completely genuine; it is opaque and can be shown inside and out. The beaker can be used to vanish articles and to exchange one item for another. It can also be used to perform a switch, that is exchanging one item for another, which appears to be identical but is in fact different.

Apparatus

You will need to purchase two identical beakers. They should be opaque, tall, and they should nest nicely one inside the other,

for this is the real secret of the trick. Place one beaker inside the other. With a small hacksaw, cut away the upper section of the top beaker so that the cut edge is now flush with the rim of the outer one. You now have an insert which sits within the main beaker and which can be removed easily, at will.

You also need several envelopes measuring approximately 162 mm × 230 mm (6 in × 9 in). Cut away and discard both top and bottom sections. Fold the remaining sections in half, lengthways, and then open out to form four-sided paper tubes. Make sure that the tubes are taller than the beaker.

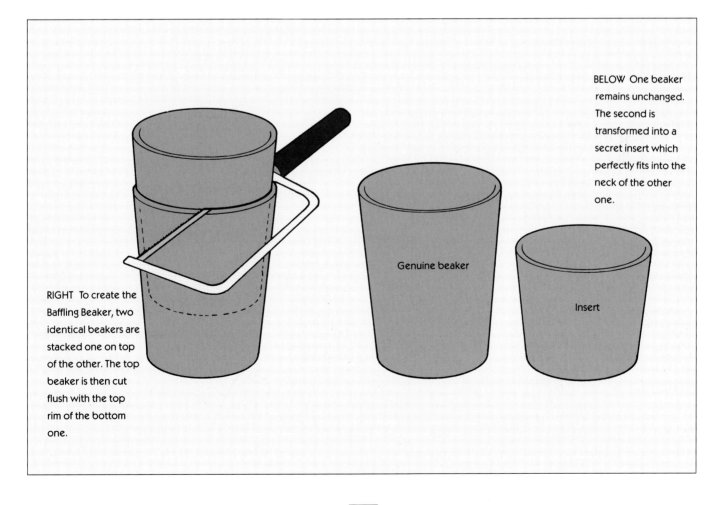

RIGHT To create the Baffling Beaker, two identical beakers are stacked one on top of the other. The top beaker is then cut flush with the top rim of the bottom one.

Genuine beaker

Insert

BELOW One beaker remains unchanged. The second is transformed into a secret insert which perfectly fits into the neck of the other one.

☆ APPARATUS ☆

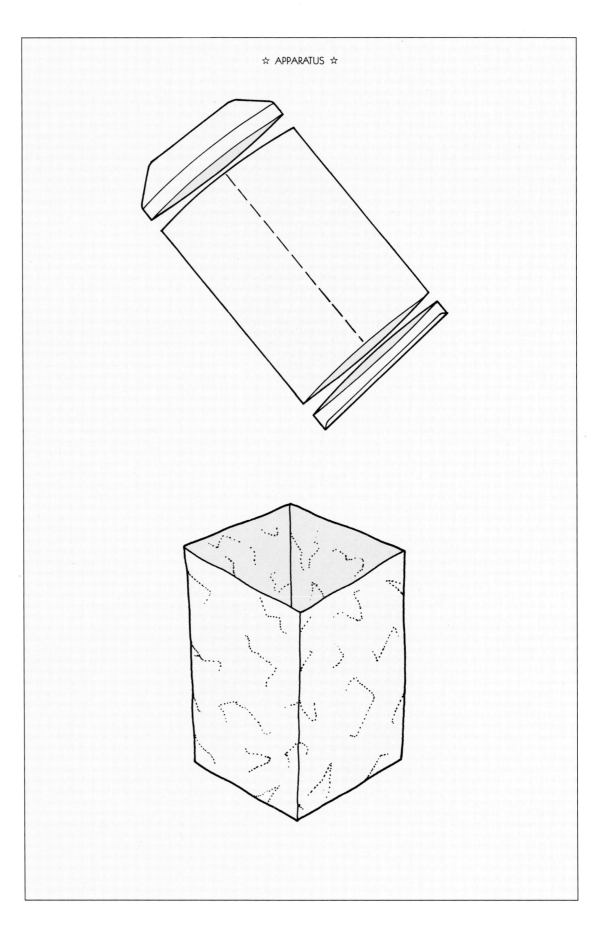

RIGHT The paper tubes are made from envelopes, with the top and bottom sections cut away, folded in half.

RIGHT The envelopes are then opened out to form four-sided tubes. The tubes must be large enough to easily fit over and completely cover the beaker.

Working and Presentation

Here are 20 examples of effects using the Baffling Beaker.

1   To vanish silk handkerchiefs: pick up the beaker and display the interior; place several handkerchiefs inside. Lift up the square tube of paper with the insert inside. Grip the insert so that it can be placed inside the beaker, covering the handkerchief. With the right hand, remove the paper tube as though it were taking something away – a rather suspicious-looking move to distract your audience. With the left hand, pick up both sections of the beakers as one and quickly show the audience the interior of the beaker (actually the insert) to reveal that the handkerchiefs have vanished. Place the beaker to one side and tear the tube into pieces, proving that it is empty.

2   In the set-up place a chain of links inside the insert beaker, and hide this in the paper tube. Display the beaker and in it place several loose paper-clips, dropping them in one at a time. Cover the beaker with the paper tube (and insert). Remove the paper tube and show that it is empty. Finally, ensure that the loose clips are trapped between the insert and the beaker, and toss the linked clips into the air.

3   In the set-up, drop some spent matches into the main beaker and put the insert on top. Drop several live matches into the beaker and cover the beaker and the insert with the paper tube. Light one further match and wave it beneath the beaker for effect. Remove the tube and the insert, and pull out several spent matches.

4   A bank note is placed inside the beaker, and the beaker is covered. The note changes into coins adding up to the denomination of the bill.

5   Pieces of coloured tissue paper magically change themselves into a Christmas decoration, which expands as it is pulled out of the beaker.

6   A safety-pin and a bolt is dropped inside the beaker. Moments later it is seen that the pin is now firmly attached to the bolt.

7   Dates taken from a calendar magically change into dates to eat.

8   A length of ribbon and several loose buttons are dropped inside the beaker. Later, the ribbon is seen to have the buttons firmly sewn onto it.

9   A loose sewing needle and a length of thread are placed into the beaker. In a matter of moments, the needle threads itself.

10   Pieces of coloured tissue paper change to a long paper streamer. After the beaker has been covered and the insert added, the beaker is inverted so that the centre of the streamer uncoils and cascades onto a table. The fingers of the hand keep the entire coil from dropping out during the production.

11   A skein of red silk magically changes into a square red silk handkerchief.

12   Two or three small silk handkerchiefs mysteriously change to a shower of confetti.

13   Water poured into the beaker instantly changes to ice cubes. (You will have to perform this trick the moment you load the ice cubes into the insert!)

14   A number of elastic bands are shown to link together in a chain. To make the chain, use flat rubber bands, making a cut in every second band. Rejoin them with a rubber cement adhesive.

15   A ball of wool magically changes into a pom-pom.

16   Steel nails are placed inside the beaker, and shaken up. When dropped onto the table, the nails are bent in half and a spectators drawn from the audience cannot bend them back to their original shape.

17   A small potato placed inside the beaker is sliced into chips. The performer makes a pretence of slicing the potato by flicking a table-knife in the air.

18   A quantity of sugar is poured into the beaker. When next the performer looks, the grains have changed into cubes.

19   Water poured into the beaker changes to rice.

20   Water poured into the beaker changes colour – to red. The paper tube covers the beaker and when the liquid is poured again, it is green. For this last effect place some red food colouring (cochineal) inside the beaker so that when water is poured into it, it changes the liquid to red. Green limeade or pure lemon juice, already inside the insert, makes the switch possible.

HITTING THE HEADLINES

· · · · ☆ ☆ ☆ · · · ·

You will certainly make the headlines in more ways than one when performing this unusual trick.

Effect

The performer takes the front page of a newspaper and draws the audience's attention to its title and the banner headline. The headline and title are ripped off and the newspaper is folded. Now for the magic! The torn section is bundled up and made to vanish. When the newspaper is reopened, it has its title and headline back in place again.

Apparatus

Two identical newspapers.

Set-up

Take one of the newspapers and carefully cut the front page down the outside fold to just beyond the title and main banner head-line. Fold this section down behind the rest of the front page, creasing firmly.

Take the second newspaper and again cut the front page down the outside fold to beyond the title and main banner headline – just a little further down than the first newspaper. Then, using a ruler as a guide, *tear* across the front page, separating the title and headline from the rest of the front page. Keep the torn-out section and discard the rest of the newspaper.

Take the torn-out title and headline, apply a little rubber solution (white) glue to the bottom reverse edge and carefully place it along the top folded edge of the first newspaper. The first newspaper now appears to be complete.

LEFT To set-up this trick, the title and headline of the first newspaper is folded behind the front page.

ABOVE The title and headline of the second identical newspaper is torn out completely. It can then be carefully pasted onto the first newspaper, so that it appears complete.

Working and Presentation

Pick up the newspaper and display it front and back. There is no need to open it at this stage of the procedure. Hold the newspaper with the right hand and with the left, 'rip' the top section off. Display the torn section and place it onto the table, and show the newspaper with its missing section. Reverse the paper so that the back is facing the audience. With the fingers of the right hand secretly pivot up the folded section inside, bringing it into view and filling in the space left by the missing portion. Fold the newspaper in half,

bringing the front of the paper inside the folds, and place this also onto the table.

The performer may wish to vanish the torn section by crumpling it into a ball using any of the sleight-of-hand methods applied to balls and other objects. Alternatively, it could be vanished in a magic box, cabinet, bag or other vanishing device.

Once the section of newspaper has been vanished, pick up the folded newspaper and open it up, turning it towards the audience to show that the title and headline have magically returned to the front page.

CAN-CAN

• • • • ☆ ☆ ☆ • • • •

The trick Passe-Passe Bottle and Glass has been a feature in the comedy acts of many magicians over the years. The version described here is just as effective although it uses items found around the home.

Effect

On the magician's table are two cardboard tubes. When these are lifted away, one reveals a can of Coke and the other a glass tumbler. The performer causes the can to change places with the tumbler, back and forth, under his command.

Apparatus

Two identical drink cans. Cut away the base of each can cleanly with a can opener and drain out the liquid. The top of the cans should remain intact. Two identical tumblers just small enough to fit inside the drink cans. Two cardboard tubes, slightly larger and taller than the drink cans. Paint the cardboard tubes with metallic paint to make them look more effective. Cut a thumb-hole towards the bottom of each tube.

Set-up

Place both tumblers on the table, approximately 30 cm (12 in) apart. Place the drink cans over the tumblers; finally, place the cardboard tubes over both units, making sure the thumb-holes are at the rear.

To reveal a drink can, simply lift up the cardboard tube. To reveal a tumbler, insert the thumb into the hole cut into the cardboard tube and lift both the tube and the can. The effect relies on the smooth operation of this manoeuvre.

Working and Presentation

Lift up both tubes at the same time, one with each hand, so that the one on your right reveals the drink can and the one on the left the tumbler. Reverse the procedure to effect the transposition and repeat at will.

RIGHT You will need *two* identical examples of each of the following (from left to right); drink can with the base cut out, glass tumbler, cardboard tube. The tumblers must fit inside the drink cans, which must in turn fit inside the cardboard tubes.

BAFFLING BALLOONS
· · · · · ☆ ☆ ☆ · · · · ·

This is an unusual effect using items that are easily obtainable.

Effect

Two paper bags are shown, one with a red spot on the front, the other sporting a green spot. They are examined by members of the audience. Two balloons are then produced, one red and one green, and dropped inside the corresponding bag. A snap of the fingers, and the red balloon is pulled from the green-spot bag and the green balloon from the red-spot bag – a neat transposition.

Apparatus

Four balloons, two of each colour, red and green; two paper bags; two coloured spots, one green and one red.

Set-up

Stick the coloured spots on the front of each of the paper bags. Push a green balloon inside a red one, using the blunt end of a pencil. Allow part of the neck of the inner balloon to protrude. The second red balloon is pushed inside the other green one in a similar fashion.

Working and Presentation

Let the audience examine the empty paper bags. Display the balloons and place them inside the bags, so that the colours of the balloons match the coloured spots. Hide the necks of the inner balloons with your fingers. Then wave a magic wand, or snap the fingers to make the effect more magical. Remove the first bag from the table, holding it firmly by the base with the fingers gripping the balloon inside through the paper. With the right hand reach inside the bag and pull out the inner balloon of a different colour. Crush the bag, containing the original outer balloon, and cast aside. Repeat with the second bag and balloon to show that both have magically transposed.

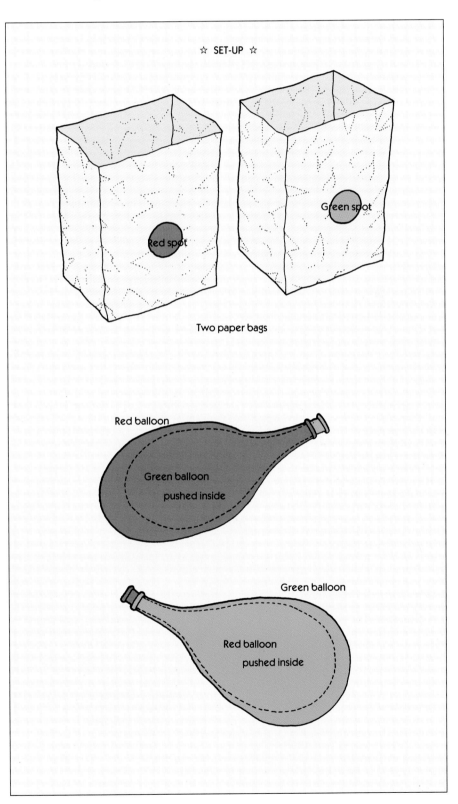

☆ SET-UP ☆

Red spot

Green spot

Two paper bags

Red balloon

Green balloon
pushed inside

Green balloon

Red balloon
pushed inside

IN BETWEEN SILK

· · · · · ☆ ☆ ☆ · · · ·

A colourful magical mystery which uses silk handkerchiefs and a flat cloth bag.

Effect

A bag is first shown empty, the performer turning it inside out. Attention is brought to the central slit cut along the base of the bag. Three silk handkerchiefs are on the table, two purple, one yellow. The performer demonstrates that a handkerchief can go into the bag from the top and can be extracted from the slit at the base. After showing the bag empty, the two purple silk handkerchiefs are placed inside. The first handkerchief is pulled out slightly at the base and the corner of the second handkerchief is pulled out to hang over the top of the bag. The yellow silk handkerchief is then loosely placed inside the bag. When the protruding corner of the purple silk is re-moved from the base, all three silks are seen to be magically tied together, the yellow one securely tied between the other two. The bag is finally shown empty.

Apparatus

A specially made cloth bag is required. As illustrated, this consists of three sections, neatly sewn together around three edges, leaving the uppermost section open. This means that the bag has two separate compartments. A slit is cut and reinforced in approximately central position towards the base of the bag, allowing access to both compartments. Six silk handkerchiefs – four purple and two yellow. Knot one yellow silk between two purple ones.

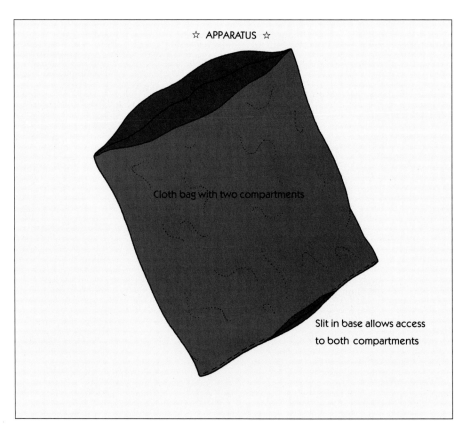

☆ APPARATUS ☆

Cloth bag with two compartments

Slit in base allows access to both compartments

Set-up

Secrete the three knotted silks in one compartment of the bag. Make sure a corner of one of the purple silks is readily available to pull through the slit at the base of the bag. The other compartment is left empty.

Working and Presentation

Turn the bag inside out to prove that it is empty. Bring the audience's attention to the three silk handkerchiefs. Display the two purple handkerchiefs and place them into the empty compartment of the bag. In doing so, almost as an afterthought – or so it would appear to the audience – pull the purple silk handkerchief through the slit in the base of the bag. In actual fact, you pull out the bottom purple silk from the other secret compartment. The same applies to the second purple silk in the secret compartment. This time, pull a corner out of the top of the bag so that it is hanging over the edge. It appears that the two loose silks which have just been placed inside have been displayed in this manner, when in reality, it is the two silk handkerchiefs which are already knotted that are on view. The third handkerchief is displayed and placed inside the bag (in the compartment which now houses the two loose silks).

Step towards a member of the audience and ask that person to pull the handkerchief out slightly at the top. Ask another spectator to gently pull the handkerchief which is protruding at the base of the bag. As each spectator pulls, they discover that the handkerchiefs become taut. When the handkerchief at the bottom of the bag is pulled out completely, the other two follow. Furthermore, both purple handkerchiefs have been on full view during the entire presentation.

Once the set of knotted silks has been removed from the bag, you can 'prove' to the audience that it is empty by turning it inside out. However, display only the compartment that is in reality now empty.

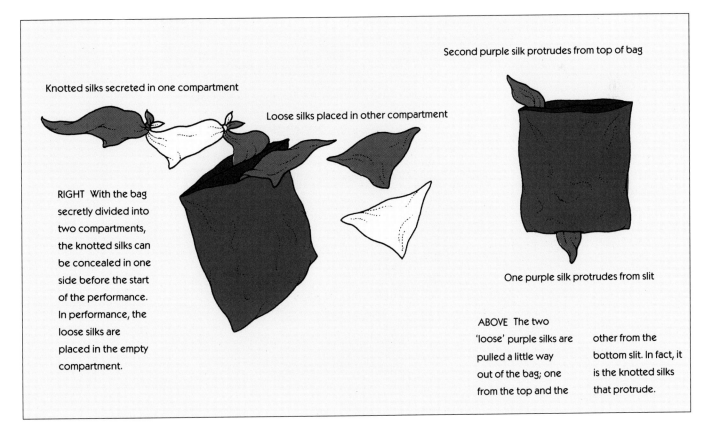

Knotted silks secreted in one compartment

Loose silks placed in other compartment

Second purple silk protrudes from top of bag

RIGHT With the bag secretly divided into two compartments, the knotted silks can be concealed in one side before the start of the performance. In performance, the loose silks are placed in the empty compartment.

One purple silk protrudes from slit

ABOVE The two 'loose' purple silks are pulled a little way out of the bag; one from the top and the other from the bottom slit. In fact, it is the knotted silks that protrude.

SPOTLESS

· · · · ☆ ☆ ☆ · · · ·

Believe it or not, this effect lends itself to performance at close quarters.

Effect

The magician shows his audience a square block painted black which he announces is a large die which has lost its spots. A small strip of white paper is next introduced. This is pleated and then rested on top of the block. To some amusing patter, the performer places a cover over both the block and folded strip. A pair of scissors is brandished, and the performer pretends to snip holes out of the paper strip by opening and closing the scissors several times. When the cover is removed, the paper strip is un-folded. Cut from the paper strip are round holes! The block is now spotted, appearing as a large six-sided die.

Apparatus

The outfit comes in three parts as illustrated. A black, solid inner block, complete with white spots to resemble a large die.

An outer shell. This consists of an open-based container which fits loosely over the spotted die. The outer surface of this shell should be black to match that of the die. The inside should also be black.

RIGHT The apparatus consists of a black, white-spotted die and a pleated strip of paper from which circular holes have been cut. This strip of paper is placed on top of the die, and this in turn is placed inside the black outer shell (as shown). A second, whole strip of pleated paper and the red outer box completes the outfit.

An outer cover. This is similar in structure to that of the shell, open at the base, but red in colour. The outer cover fits over both the shell and the solid die.

Two strips of white paper. One is left untouched, except that it is pleated. The duplicate has cut-out holes running down its length. This strip of paper should also be pleated.

Set-up

Place the solid die on the table or onto a plate or tray. Place the pleated strip of paper which has holes cut from it, on top of the die. Place the shell over both so that you now appear to have a solid black block on

display. Position the outer cover and the whole paper strip near-by.

Working and Presentation

Display the black block together with the strip of paper, unfolding it to show that it is intact. Refold it and place it on top of the black block, placing the cover over both. Remove the cover together with the inner shell (and the paper strip that is wedged between) to reveal the block covered with white spots. The pleated paper is unfolded to show that cut-out holes run down its entire length. Before removing the cover, you can snip a pair of scissors in the air several times, for visual effect.

ABOVE To reveal the concealed spotted die, the red box *and* the black shell are lifted away together.

MENTAL MYSTERIES

Whether or not you believe in mind-reading, many audiences are fascinated by mentalist experiments. The fact is, however, that it is all trickery.

Most mentalists like to call their performances experiments. One good reason for using this term is that while tricks should never go wrong, some experiments can, and it is easy to blame a failure on the atmosphere or the unsuitability of a particular member of the audience.

Never mix mentalist experiments with other kinds of tricks or with comedy routines. The mentalist should style himself a specialist, because part of the effect stems from the audience's belief that the performer is a special kind of person. The mentalist should have clear diction and a powerful voice. He or she should be upright and commanding – a person worthy of the respect due to one who can read minds and tell the future. Use concise patter, avoiding comedy. Experiments should always be clear and dramatic in presentation, and the results baffling and entertaining.

PERPLEXING PENS

· · · · · ☆ ☆ ☆ · · · · ·

Simple, everyday props and a dramatic presentation serve to produce a puzzling mind-reading test.

Effect

The performer reveals that when the three caps of three identical ballpoint pens are removed, and when spectators use the pens on paper, each has a different coloured ink; one is red, one is blue, and one is black. The pens are laid down onto the table and mixed by anyone who wishes to become involved in the experiment. This can be done while the performer turns away or is blindfolded. One pen is freely selected by a member of the audience and handed to the performer. Without seeing the pen he states the colour of its ink. The performer is always correct and the effect can be repeated over and over again.

Apparatus

Three pens. These should be plastic ball-point pens with opaque, not transparent, casings. Make sure that all casings and caps are of the same colour, but they must contain inks of three different colours.

Working and Presentation

Display the three pens and ask a spectator to test them out, scribbling on the note-pad. Ensure that the audience see that although the three pens look identical, their inks are of different colours. Ask the spectator to re-place the caps and mix up the pens before replacing them onto the table. You can be blindfolded at this point, or simply turn away from the audience.

Ask the spectator to freely choose one of the three pens, and hand it to you. Now turn to face the audience, and at this point quickly execute the important move. Behind your back, using both hands, quickly uncap the pen, then stroke the ballpoint end across your thumbnail so as to leave a trace of the colour behind. Quickly replace the cap and bring the pen out towards the front, holding it up for all to see. Recap the points of the effect to the audience. Hand the chosen pen to the spectator. Remove the blindfold then glance at your thumbnail to spot the chosen colour. Divine the colour and ask the spectator to confirm that it is right.

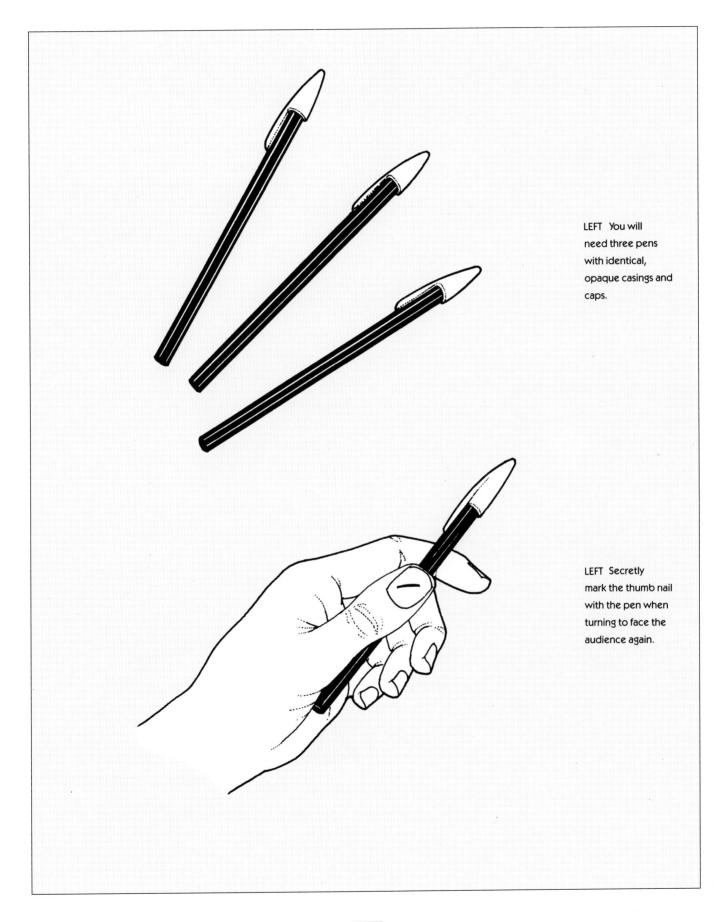

LEFT You will need three pens with identical, opaque casings and caps.

LEFT Secretly mark the thumb nail with the pen when turning to face the audience again.

DUPLICATED DIVINATION

· · · · ☆ ☆ ☆ · · · ·

A mental effect which can be presented impromptu or as part of the mentalist's programme.

Effect

The performer displays two cardboard boxes, each with a removable lid. Both boxes are identical in every way – size, shape and colour. Inside each box is an identical wooden block. Not only are these identical in shape, size and colour but the designs on all six sides are also the same. We use ESP symbols: the star, wavy lines, square, circle and cross, with the addition of a triangle to make up the six.

The performer retains one of the boxes containing one of the blocks, and the spectator takes control of the other. The spectator is requested to remove the block, look at one of the symbols and concentrate on it. It is a free selection and he can change his mind if he so wishes. The performer turns his back to the audience while the choice is being made so he cannot see the movements of the spectator.

Once the spectator has made a definite choice he is asked to place the block inside the box, with the chosen design uppermost so that he cannot change his mind at this stage. The lid is replaced, and the box returned to the table.

The performer now turns to face his audience. He removes his block, displays it, thinks carefully and then places it inside with a particular design facing uppermost. When another spectator checks both boxes and their contents, he finds that the uppermost designs are identical. The blocks and boxes can be examined by all.

Apparatus

Two small cardboard boxes, measuring approximately 5 cm (2 in) square. Each has a removable fit-on, flanged lid. Both should be identical in appearance.

Two blocks. These should fit the boxes snugly but should slide out smoothly when required. They should be black, and each of the six sides should be illustrated in white with a different ESP symbol. Both blocks are identical in that the designs appear on the same sides.

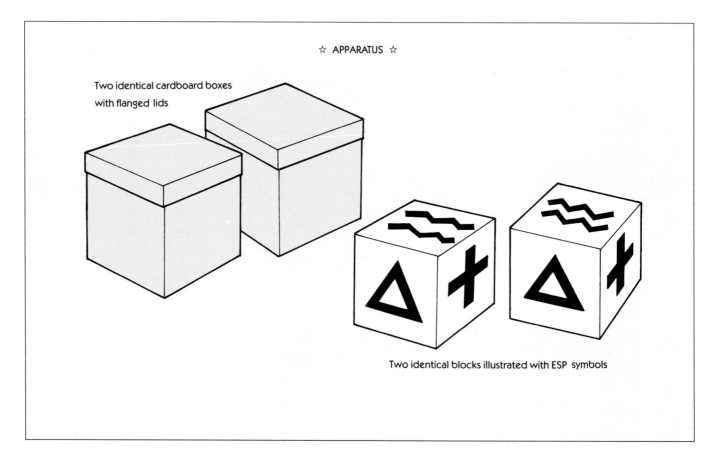

☆ APPARATUS ☆

Two identical cardboard boxes with flanged lids

Two identical blocks illustrated with ESP symbols

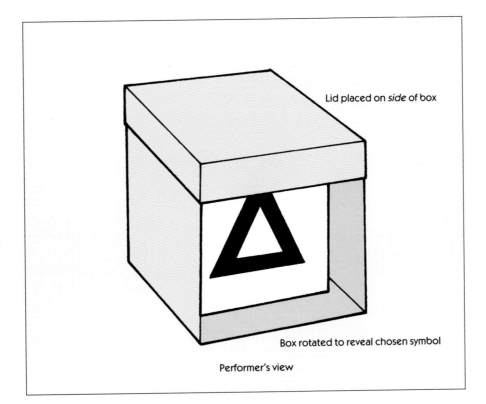

Lid placed on *side* of box

Box rotated to reveal chosen symbol

Performer's view

RIGHT The secret to this trick lies not in the performer's ability to read minds, but in his ability to handle the props. See the text for the final explanation.

Set-up

Simply put the blocks inside their boxes and place the lids on top.

Working and Presentation

Explain to the audience that it is sometimes possible to have duplicate thoughts – two people thinking of the same thing at the same time. Display both boxes, and ask a spectator to examine them. Draw attention towards the fact that each contains a similar block with identical ESP symbols. Ask the spectator to choose one symbol, and to place the block in the box so that the chosen symbol is uppermost, retaining an image of it in his mind. As a necessary precaution against seeing any of the spectator's movements during this important stage of the experiment, turn away.

When the box has been closed, turn to face the audience and recap on what has taken place so far. In doing so, pick up the spectator's box and hold it behind your back. It is at this point that the vital move is made. Out of view of the audience, rotate

the lid and slide it down one side of the box. Then rotate the whole box so that it looks to the audience as if the lid is still on top and bring the box in front. The chosen face of the block inside the box is now visible to you but not to the audience. Glance at the symbol that is showing and put the box on the table.

Now go to the second box and make a show of reading the thoughts of the spectator, turning the block this way and that, finally placing it inside its box with the correct pattern uppermost. This being done, all that remains is to reopen both boxes and prove the divination is correct. Pick up the spectator's box, and in one swift but casual movement cup the right hand over the lid and pull it away, allowing the left hand to rotate the box upwards so that the base of it now rests on the palm of the left hand. This rotation should not be detectable to the audience. Remove the lid so that the audience can see the chosen design on top. Request the spectator to open the lid of your box to reveal the identical design.

A BAFFLING BOOK TEST

· · · · ☆ ☆ ☆ · · · ·

Magicians and mentalists alike have been using book tests for more years than I can remember. While methods vary, the effect still always seems to remain the same.

LEFT A book, a marker and a willing spectator is all that is needed to perform the Baffling Book Test.

Effect

A paperback book of some 180 pages is used. It could be one belonging to a member of the audience, proving that the book itself is genuine. The performer flicks through the pages, informing the audience that there must surely be hundreds of words on each page. He hands the book to a spectator, requesting that he or she flicks through the book to find a page of their choice. The spectator is requested to look at the very last word on that particular page. The performer's business card, or perhaps a playing card is inserted between the pages to mark the selection. This is all done by the spectator; the performer has turned his or her back. The mentalist, of course, reveals the page number and the last word on the page.

Apparatus

A paperback book; a business or playing card to be used as a marker.

Working and Presentation

Hand the book to a spectator, asking him to flick through the pages so that it can be verified to your audience that each page is different. Also ask him or her to verify the fact that the book is not prepared in any way. Hand over the business or playing card and ask the spectator to turn to a page of his choice and remember the number. Next, ask him to remember the last word on that page and insert the business card to act as a marker. Reclaim the book from the spectator.

While the business card is there to act as a marker, it is also there to assist you in obtaining vital information required: the page number and the last word on the chosen page. This is how it works.

In recapping what has been done so far, riffle through the pages of the book, saying that it must contain thousands of words. As you do this, you will find that your thumb stops briefly at the position where the card is inserted. The thumb jumps, landing on the page next to it. In that brief second, note both the page number at the bottom and the last word of the page, then continue to flick through the remaining pages. The whole procedure should be presented as if you are simply establishing the fact that the book contains 180 pages and thousands of words.

The rest of the experiment is easy. Ask the spectator to concentrate on the page number and last word, and divine both.

HOW MANY?

· · · · ☆ ☆ ☆ · · · ·

If you had six matchboxes, each filled with a different number of matches, and these were all mixed up while you were out of the room, would you be able to tell your audience just how many matches were inside the box freely chosen by a spectator?

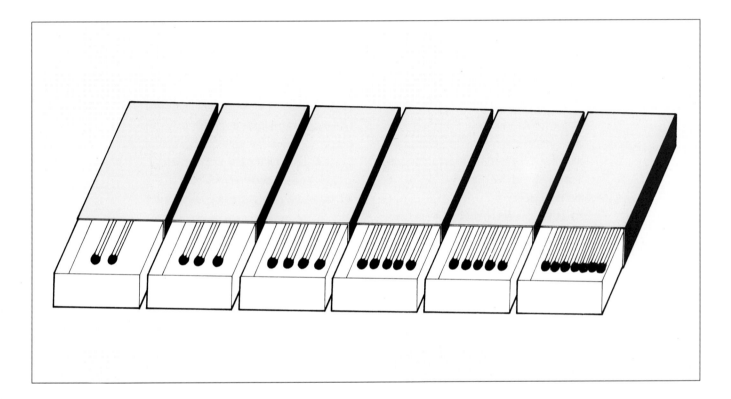

Apparatus

Six identical matchboxes; matches; a paper bag. The number of matches inside each of the boxes can be of your own selection although it is unwise to go into high numbers. I suggest you set up your six boxes with the following number of matchsticks in each: 2, 3, 4, 5, 6, and 7.

Set-up

The matches should be inside the boxes and the paper bag should be placed nearby.

Working and Presentation

Display all six matchboxes, and allow the spectators to open them. Bring to their attention the fact that no two matchboxes contain the same number of matches. At this stage turn your back to the audience, or leave the room – first leaving instructions for the following stages. Ask a spectator to close the matchboxes. Mix them up well, and hand each to a different spectator. He then chooses one of the spectators, who then opens his box, counts the matches inside and closes it again.

Re-enter the room or turn around, and ask which spectator is holding the selected matchbox. Now pick up the paper bag in your left hand and take each matchbox in turn with the right hand, dropping it into the paper bag. When you come to the selected box, open it slightly as you drop it into the bag. When all six boxes have been placed inside the bag, crumple up the top and ask a spectator to give it a good shake.

Next, begin the divination. Pick the first box out of the bag and place it against your forehead, appearing to concentrate hard. Pronounce that this is not the box you are looking for. Do the same with the next couple of boxes. When you remove the box that is part opened, glance at the opened end and quickly count the matches that are showing. Close the box before it comes into view of the audience, put it to one side of the others and extract the remaining boxes.

Pronounce the number of matches inside the chosen box you have put to one side of the others, and then prove that your divination is indeed correct.

MATCH THAT!

· · · · · ☆ ☆ ☆ · · · ·

Who would like to play a game of match-that! This is not a child's game, however, but an experiment which elicits the attention of those members of an audience who are looking for something different.

Effect

The performer declares to the audience that he is holding a pack of cards made up of matching pairs. He hands them to a member of the audience to shuffle, then selects one card at random and seals it inside an envelope, without showing the face to the audience. The performer then fans the cards face-up so that the audience can see that the pack contains two of each card. He closes up the pack, places the sealed envelope on top and asks the spectator to sign the envelope. Removing the envelope, the performer asks another spectator to cut the pack. He then places the envelope on top of the bottom stack – to mark the cut – and places the top stack on top of the envelope.

The performer announces that it would be a very strange coincidence if the card he randomly selected and sealed in an envelope and the card the spectator freely cut at were in fact a matching pair. Sure enough both cards are indeed identical.

Apparatus

A pack consisting of 27 pairs of cards; an envelope.

Working and Presentation

Hand the pack to a member of the audience to shuffle. Take the cards back and randomly select one card; glance at the face quickly as you seal it in the envelope. Fan the cards face-up to the audience so that they can inspect the pack, but note the position of the card matching the one in the envelope. In closing up the pack, secretly cut it so that the duplicate card is the top card of the pack (all the cards are face down). Rest the envelope on top of the pack and ask a spectator to sign it to prove that it is genuine; this is a deliberate misdiretion. On removing the envelope from the pack, secretly take away the top card as well. Ask a second spectator to cut the pack, then mark the cut by sandwiching the envelope (and the hidden card) between the two stacks – the duplicate card is now in the cut-at position. Ask the first spectator to part the pack, take the envelope and remove the card, placing it face-down on the table. Ask the second spectator to remove the cut-at card on top of the bottom stack and place it face down beside the first. Finally, reverse both cards to show that they are a matching pair.

THE ILLUSION SHOW

The creation of illusions requires large-scale apparatus, a more spacious performing area (say, a stage or platform), and the help of an assistant. The equipment required for a professional illusion show can be expensive, but here are a number of illusions which can be performed effectively with the minimum of outlay.

The illusionist's assistant is a very important person. It is often the case that the assistant performs the illusion, while the performer simply makes the presentation. Assistants should be well turned-out and should carry themselves confidently. They should rehearse with the performer to ensure that vital points of timing are correct.

It is possible to combine illusions with other tricks and effects. A professional illusion show can introduce not only male and female assistants, but also lions and tigers, eagles and doves, and in some cases, an elephant or two!

Over 60 years after his death, Harry Houdini is still renowned as the great illusionist who could escape from any type of bond -- handcuffs, straightjackets, ropes (as seen here), and even boxes chained and submerged in water. One of his early illusions was a stunning sack escape involving a transposition – for a simplified version see the Sensational Sack Escape.

CHILDREN WILL NEED SUPERVISION

SENSATIONAL SACK ESCAPE

· · · · ☆ ☆ ☆ · · · ·

Master escapologist Harry Houdini freed himself from chains, padlocks and sacks as no other escape artiste could. Houdini became a household name during his lifetime, and even to this day the public still remember him. Although easy to make and put into practice, this sack escape is just as baffling as those enacted by Harry Houdini.

Effect

The performer requests two spectators to come forward and assist in preparing the illusion. First, a canvas sack is examined, in-side and out. Next, the performer climbs into the bag, ducks down inside and asks the spectators to tie the rope which is threaded through holes in the top hem of the bag. Several knots are tied firmly so that the performer is securely encased within the sack. A folding screen is erected in front of the performer in the sack. Both spectators retire to their seats and one is asked to time the escape.

Within one minute the performer is seen to have escaped from the sack as he moves the screen to one side and offers the sack for examination.

Apparatus

A canvas sack large enough to hold a human. One that is made out of black canvas is most suitable. Several holes are cut along the top hem of the bag (these can be grommeted for better wear) so that a length of rope may be threaded through. There should be *plenty* of rope left at each end of the threaded piece. A folding screen or curtain that is easily transported.

Set-up

The folding screen should be upright with the sack hanging over the top.

Working and Presentation

While one spectator could in fact do all the work for you, the second spectator makes the illusion look much more difficult to

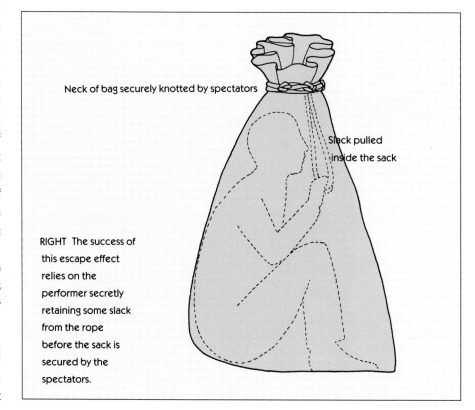

Neck of bag securely knotted by spectators

Slack pulled inside the sack

RIGHT The success of this escape effect relies on the performer secretly retaining some slack from the rope before the sack is secured by the spectators.

accomplish, since the tying and checking of the sack should appear to be most impor-tant. The spectators examine the sack, place it on the floor, and then peel back the sides so that the inside base is on view. Stand on the base and ask the spectators to bring up the sides of the sack; at the same time lower one hand slightly and duck inside. It is at this stage that you execute the one important move which makes the illusion work. Since plenty of rope was threaded around the neck of the sack, as you duck down, pull in some slack, holding this down firmly. As the spectators pull the length of rope tightly to close the sack, retain a firm grip of the slack

inside. The spectators can tie as many knots as they wish around the top of the bag. The spectators then erect the folding screen in front of the sack and return to their seats.

It only takes a matter of seconds to escape from the sack, but getting a member of the audience to time you makes for good showmanship and a better presentation. To accomplish the escape, release tension on the slack, push open the top, peel the sack down, and step out. You could deliberately prolong the presentation by making noises as though struggling to free yourself. Once free, throw the sack over the screen and make your appearance.

CHILDREN WILL NEED SUPERVISION

ROD THROUGH BODY

· · · · ☆ ☆ ☆ · · · ·

Penetrating swords, rods and canes through assistants encased inside a cabinet is one thing, but pushing a solid metal rod through a spectator's body without the aid of cabinets or concealment of any kind is another.

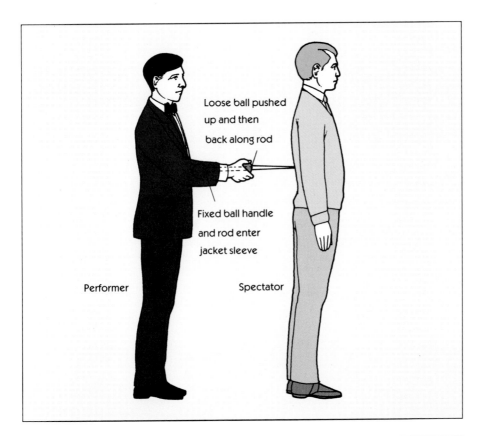

Loose ball pushed up and then back along rod

Fixed ball handle and rod enter jacket sleeve

Performer   Spectator

Effect

A spectator is asked to examine a solid rod of steel. The rod is approximately 40 cm (15 in) long with an attached ball handle at one end. Once examined, it is returned to the performer who requests another spectator to come onto the stage and stand side on to the audience.

Immediately, and without any cover, the performer magically pushes the steel rod through the spectator's back. The rod is extracted and handed out to the audience for thorough examination. The amazing thing about this version is that only one rod is used, eliminating switches of any kind.

Apparatus

A solid rod of steel, approximately 40 cm (15 in) long for best effect. The end of the rod is tapered to give the appearance of a more dangerous weapon. A solid wooden ball is firmly attached to the opposite end of the rod. You will require two such wooden balls. These must be identical in appearance. Bore a hole halfway into one of the balls and force it tightly onto the untapered end of the rod. A spot of contact adhesive can be applied so that the ball becomes part of the unit and acts as a handle. The duplicate wooden ball should also be drilled, producing a hole slightly larger than that of the

diameter of the rod. Both balls should be painted red. An added touch is to doctor a special white pocket handkerchief with red marks representing blood stains, so that when the material of the handkerchief is folded, the stains are not on view. You must wear a jacket to perform this illusion.

Set-up

Place the duplicate loose red ball handle, together with the pocket handkerchief, inside the right jacket pocket. The rod should be placed on the table.

Working and Presentation

Select a spectator for the illusion – he or she is called the victim – but assure the audience that at no time is there any danger involved. Hand the steel rod to the spectator for examination, and (for dramatic effect) whack it down on top of the table, proving it is solid. Remove the handkerchief from the right jacket pocket saying you may need it if there is a 'slight accident'. At the same time, secrete the loose ball within the right palm. Place the handkerchief, which has now served its purpose, to one side, and at the same time secretly slip the palmed ball onto the tapered end of the rod.

Ask the spectator to take his position, standing sideways on in front of the audience, and while he does this, secretly push the duplicate ball down the rod towards the opposite end, so that it rests against the fixed one. Holding the loose ball handle and working with the right-hand side of the body towards the audience, prod the tapered end of the rod into the centre of the spectator's back. The loose ball handle is the only one on view – the fixed one is concealed behind the right arm. Push the loose handle along the rod, allowing the fixed handle and the rod to enter inside the right jacket sleeve. It appears to the audience that the rod is actually penetrating the spectator's body. Push the loose handle along the entire length of the rod and then pull it slowly back again allowing the rod to reappear from the jacket sleeve – do not reveal the fixed handle, however.

Now pick up the pocket handkerchief, cover the loose ball and rub the handkerchief along the length of the rod; as it comes towards the tapered end, so too does the loose ball. Secretly drop the loose ball into the waiting left hand – this side of the body is away from the audience. Place the rod on the table and open out the pocket handkerchief to show the artificial blood stains. Discard both the pocket handkerchief and the hidden ball in the left pocket and the rod can be examined once more.

TWO-TUBES ILLUSION

· · · · ☆ ☆ ☆ · · · ·

Most illusions are based on old methods. This particular effect relies on a principle which is still much used even to this day – black art. The principle is that black objects are invisible against a black background.

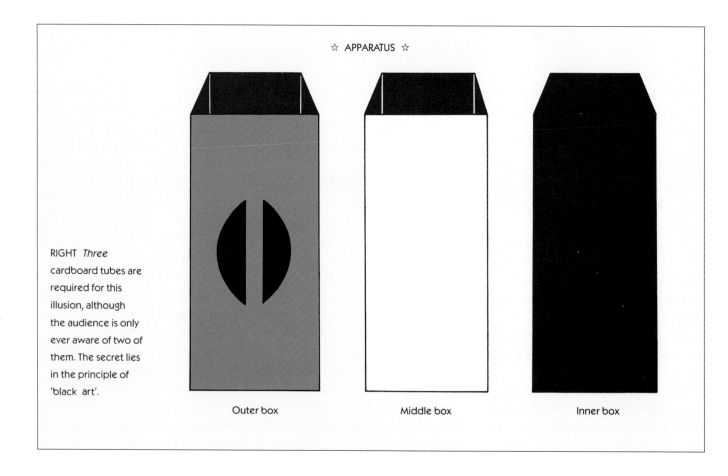

☆ APPARATUS ☆

RIGHT *Three* cardboard tubes are required for this illusion, although the audience is only ever aware of two of them. The secret lies in the principle of 'black art'.

Outer box   Middle box   Inner box

☆ SET-UP ☆

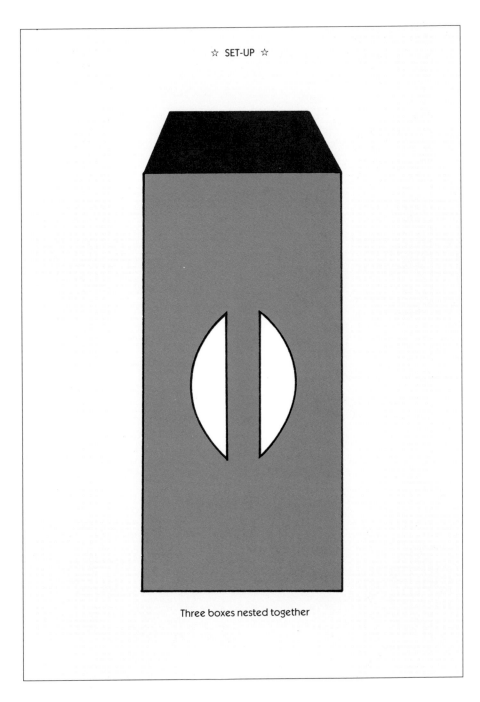

Three boxes nested together

With a sharp cutting knife, cut out a decorative portion from the largest of the three boxes; this will be the outer box. Paint this box red on the outside. Leave the middle box whole but paint it yellow on the outside. Paint the interiors of both boxes matt black. Paint the third and smallest box – the inner box – matt black inside and out, and attach a length of black velveteen to the front panel with staples or glue. A flap of velveteen should be left at the top and brought over the open top of the box.

Set-up

The three boxes are nested together with the inner black box containing the assistant crouched down inside. The length of black cloth is brought over the top of the box, covering the assistant's head.

Working and Presentation

During this illusion the audience are only aware that two tubes are being used. The third and smallest tube is hidden by the black art principle. To create the illusion that both tubes are empty, first pull up the outer red tube and display the open top end towards the audience so that they can see the black interior. Replace the tube on top of the yellow tube again. Remove the inner yellow tube from the nest – it can be seen through the cut-out shapes of the red tube, pulling it up and away. The cut-out segments of the outer red tube appear to show through into the matt black interior but actually reveal the black velveteen-covered inner box. Both boxes appear empty but a certain amount of misdirection should be introduced when displaying this second tube – all eyes should be on your movements. Replace the yellow tube.

The assistant now peels the loose section of black cloth from his or her head and tucks it down inside the front of the box. Then fire the blank pistol and the assistant leaps out of both boxes. Fold all three boxes (including the hidden piece of cloth) flat.

Effect

Two large tubes are shown to be empty. They are nested together. A fire of a pistol brings about a dramatic shot, and from inside the tubes an assistant is produced.

Apparatus

Three large cardboard tubes, one piece of velveteen cloth and a cutting knife. You also need red, yellow and matt black paint, a brush and a blank cartridge gun (optional). Try to obtain three cardboard boxes of the type used to package electrical appliances, such as a washing machine, a cooker or a refrigerator. These come in all shapes and sizes, but it is important that you find three which nest together – you may need to cut and trim sections of the box to achieve this. Remove the tops and bottoms of the boxes to create the tubes.

FOLDING SCREEN PRODUCTION

· · · · · ☆ ☆ ☆ · · · · ·

Effect

The illusionist displays two folding screens, folding each flat before erecting them upright, forming a cabinet. The performer places a small stool next to the screens and stands on it, reaching inside to first produce all sorts of things, then stepping down to remove the screens to reveal an assistant.

Apparatus

Two two-leaf folding screens, approximately 1.8 m (6 ft) high; a small stool; a large cloth filled with various items for production – the cloth is attached to cords so that it can hang around the assistant's neck.

Set-up

At the start of the performance, both screens are upright, opened out at the same angle, and are positioned about a metre (a few feet) apart. The assistant is hidden behind screen A. Hanging from his or her neck is the cloth bag which contains items to be produced. The small stool should be nearby.

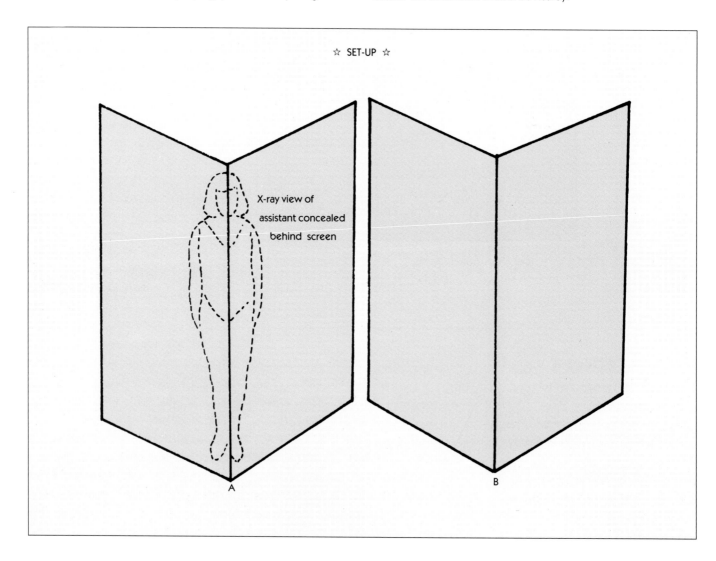

☆ SET-UP ☆

X-ray view of assistant concealed behind screen

A

B

Working and Presentation

Although the method employed is a simple one, the secret here is to time all movements carefully so that the displaying and erection of the screens appears natural and smooth. It is therefore most important for both the performer and assistant to rehearse the sequences thoroughly before presentation to an audience.

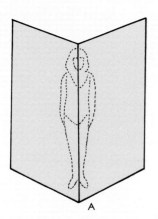

1 Display screen B by first folding it flat and showing both faces to the audience.

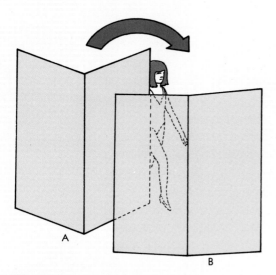

2 Then, open it out so that both panels are fully extended, allowing one leaf to overlap the edge of screen A. At this point the assistant behind screen A secretly moves out and in behind screen B.

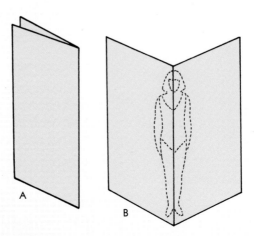

3 Now, set screen B at an angle so that it stands upright with the assistant hidden behind it and display screen A to the audience.

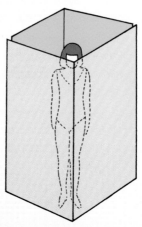

4 Place screen A on the opposite side of screen B to form an enclosed cabinet of sorts, with the assistant secretly encased within this set-up.

☆ THE PRODUCTION ☆

Stand on the small stool to reach inside the cabinet, and with the help of the assistant produce the items from the cloth bag. For a smooth performance, the assistant should hand up items in quick succession. Finally, produce the cloth so that the assistant is left absolutely clean before his or her appearance, and part the folding screens to reveal the assistant.

BIBLIOGRAPHY

It is not usually possible to find books on magic on the shelves of general bookshops or in public libraries. There are a number of specialist publishing houses that only publish books about conjuring, and they sell by mail-order or at magicians' conventions.

★ BOOKS ★

Adair, Ian *Encyclopedia of Dove Magic,* vols 1–5 (Supreme Magic Company Ltd, Bideford, North Devon, latest edition 1987). Over a period of two decades the author has gathered together the ultimate in dove magic with the best effects of the leading dove workers throughout the world.

Adair, Ian *Knowhow Book of Jokes and Tricks* (Usborne Publishing Ltd, London, 1977). A paperback designed for children. Cartoon illustrations and easy-to-follow text describe simple yet effective magical tricks and joke items.

Adair, Ian *Magic Step-by-Step* (Arco Publishing Company Inc, New York, 1972). Aimed at the beginner, with tips and advice on all aspects of conjuring, plus a wide selection of magical effects.

Adair, Ian *Television Card Manipulations* (Supreme Magic Company Ltd, Bideford, North Devon, 1962). A small book outlining the correct techniques used to produce, vanish, change and manipulate playing cards.

Bobo, J B *The New Modern Coin Magic Book* (Magic Inc, Chicago, 1966). A complete work on the manipultion and techniques used in coin magic.

Booth, John *The John Booth Classics* (Supreme Magic Company Ltd, Bideford, North Devon, 1975). The author's three major books amalgamated in one publication.

Braue, Fred and Hugard, Jean *Royal Road to Card Magic* (Dover Publications, New York, 1980). Accepted as the card-workers' bible, here is a step-by-step course in card conjuring.

Fox, Karrell *Clever Like a Fox* (Supreme Magic Company Ltd, Bideford, North Devon, 1976). Clever and original magical effects from one of the USA's leading comedy magic performers.

Fox, Karrell *My Latest Book* (Supreme Magic Company Ltd, Bideford, North Devon, 1987). The latest in his series, Fox (the author of some ten magical books) offers readers yet another selection of the type of magical notions for which he is famous.

Ganson, Lewis *Art of Close-up Magic* vols 1 & 2 (Supreme Magic Company Ltd, Bideford North Devon, 1970). Brilliant close-up magic designed for impromptu work.

Ganson, Lewis *Card Magic by Manipulation* (Supreme Magic Company Ltd, Bideford, North Devon, 1971). A small book dealing with the production and vanish of playing cards when manipulated in the hands.

Clark, Keith *Encyclopedia of Cigarette Magic* (Tannens, New York, 1952). The countless methods, the many gadgets used and the hundreds of sleight of hand moves which make possible the production of cigarettes from the fingertips.

Corinda, Tony *Thirteen Steps to Mentalism* (Supreme Magic Company Ltd, Bideford, North Devon, 1978). Acclaimed as one of the finest books to cover the branch of mental magic. In 13 steps, the author discusses predictions, divinations, ESP mysteries, and telepathic experiments.

Gibson, Walter *The Complete Illustrated Book of Card Magic* (Kaye & Ward Ltd, London, 1970). A large illustrated volume which provides the reader with countless card tricks, some easy, some more advanced.

Hooper, Edwin *Edwin's Magic* vols 1 & 2 (Edwin's Magic Arts, Bideford, North Devon, 1989). Two superb volumes by the founder of the largest magic dealing firm.

McComb, Billy *McComb's Magic – 25 Years Wiser* (Supreme Magic Company Ltd, Bideford, North Devon, 1972). Professional magician McComb, now working in Hollywood, shares his very best magic secrets.

Pavel *The Magic of Pavel* (Supreme Magic Company Ltd, Bideford, North Devon, 1970). Original conceptions from one of magic's most prolific magical inventors.

Rice, Harold *Rice's Encyclopedia of Silk Magic* vols 1–3 (Silk King Studios, Cincinnati, 1962). Magic using silk handkerchiefs of all sizes and colours.

Stickland, William G *Introducing Bill's Magic* (Supreme Magic Company Ltd, Bideford, North Devon, 1970). Unusual originations using new principles.

Tarbell, Harlan *Tarbell Course in Magic* (D Robbins & Co Inc, New York, 1980). Possibly the greatest course in magic ever published.

★ MAGAZINES ★

Abracadabra Ed. Donald Bevan (Goodliffe Publications Ltd, Bromsgrove, Worcestershire). A well-established weekly which covers all aspects of magic including tricks, patter presentations, book reviews, society reports, news, views and topics on the magic scene. Includes a varied selection of advertisements from the world's leading magic dealers.

Alakazam Ed. Maurice Day (Supreme Magic Company Ltd, Bideford, North Devon). A bi-monthly magazine of magic designed for the children's entertainer.

Info Ed. Dennis Patten (International Magic Studio, London). A glossy bi-monthly magazine which publishes a general assortment of magical effects, from close-up to illusions.

The Genii Ed. Bill Larsen (Genii, Los Angeles). A monthly glossy magazine which is well established in its field.

The Magigram Ed. Ken de Courcy (Supreme Magic Company Ltd, Bideford, North Devon). The contents are varied with effects and routines for all types of magic performers – close-up workers, children's entertainers, mentalists, escapologists, balloon modellers and illusionists.

The Tops Ed. Gordon Miller (Abbott's Manufacturing Company, Colon). An American monthly house magazine created by the founder of the company, Percy Abbott. The contents include reports, gossip, trick cartoons, illusion plans and a wide selection of magical effects and routines.

Trixigram Ed. Ian Adair (Supreme Magic Company Ltd, Bideford, North Devon). This monthly periodical contains news and views on what is happening on the magic scene throughout the world.

GLOSSARY OF TERMS

BACK-PALM To conceal an object at the back of the hand.

BLACK ART The principle that black upon black shows no join, or that black upon black is invisible.

BOOK TEST In mentalism, a demonstration in which the performer divines or predicts a freely chosen passage in a book or magazine handled by a spectator.

BOTTOM CARD The card whose face can be seen when the pack is assembled. Also called the face card.

BOTTOM DEAL The secret dealing of the bottom card of the pack, instead of the top card.

BOTTOM STOCK That portion of a pack of cards which is at the bottom when cut.

BREAK A small gap held at the edge of a pack of cards, and maintained (usually by the tip of a finger).

BRIDGE A gap in a pack of cards caused by bending some cards.

C & R Abbreviation for cut and restored, usually applied to tricks in which a rope, string, thread or tape is cut and mended.

CHANGING BAG A bag with two (or more) compartments, used for exchanging one article for another.

CONJURER'S CHOICE No choice at all. See also FORCE.

CRIMP To secretly bend one corner of a card.

CUT To divide a pack of cards into two or more sections. A complete cut is made when the sections are reassembled.

DROP To drop the balance of cards held in the hand during the shuffle so that they fall upon the shuffled cards.

EFFECT Description of trick as seen by the audience.

END GRIP Manner of holding a pack of cards with the thumb at one end and fingers at the other.

ESCAPOLOGY The art and craft of the magician who specializes in escaping from handcuffs, ropes and other restraints.

ESP Abbreviation for extra-sensory perception, which includes mind-reading, clairvoyance and kindred phenomena achieved by unrecognized physical means.

ESP CARDS Specially designed cards, used for ESP experiments. There are five designs: circle, cross, wavy lines, square and star. A pack of 25 cards contains five of each design. Apart from genuine ESP experiments, they are now widely used by conjurers.

FACE CARD See BOTTOM CARD.

FAIR SHUFFLE A genuine shuffle of the cards, as compared to false shuffle.

FAKE A piece of apparatus that has been secretly prepared for trickery.

FALSE COUNT Method of counting cards, coins, etc, so as to show there to be more or less than their real number.

FALSE SHUFFLE Method of apparently shuffling a pack of cards without changing the order of some or all of the cards.

FIRST CARD The top card of the pack when the cards are held face down, or the first card to be dealt, whether face-up or face-down.

FORCE To restrict a spectator's choice to a single item when he believes he has a choice of more than one.

KEY CARD A card in some way distinctive so that it can be recognized by the magician.

KNIFE FORCE Method of forcing a card on a spectator by having him thrust a table knife into the pack. Manipulation then brings the forced card into position above or below the knife blade.

LOAD An article, or collection of articles, prepared so that it can be secretly inserted into a container for production later.

MENTALISM The branch of conjuring involving alleged mind-reading, clairvoyance, divination, etc, but using practical and physical means to achieve what appear to be psychic results.

MISDIRECTION The art of diverting the spectator's attention at the critical moment of a trick.

MOVE The manipulation required to perform a trick.

OVERHAND SHUFFLE The normal way of shuffling cards in Britain, in which the cards held edgeways in the left hand are picked up and replaced in batches by the right hand (or vice versa if left-handed).

PALM To conceal an object secretly in the hand, not necessarily by a convulsive clutch in the actual palm.

PRODUCTION The production of articles from a supposedly empty container, or from thin air.

REVERSED CARD A playing card that is returned to the pack either back to front or upside down.

RIFFLE SHUFFLE To shuffle a pack, divided into two equal stacks, by interlacing the cards. A number of modern card tricks depend upon this being done with total accuracy. Very considerable skill is required.

ROPE CEMENT An adhesive, sometimes used for joining two pieces of rope.

SET-UP The prearrangement of apparatus.

SIDE-GRIP The practice of holding a pack of cards by its long edges.

SLEEVE To secretly insert an article in the sleeve.

SLEIGHT The secret manipulation required to perform a trick.

SQUARE To adjust the edges of a pack of cards by pressing them into alignment with fingers and thumb after the cards have been shuffled, for example.

STAGE MONEY Imitation bank notes and treasury bills, used for stage pruposes including conjuring.

STOCK The main portion of a pack of cards as opposed to those being immediately dealt or otherwise used for playing or magical purpose.

SWITCH To imperceptibly exchange one article for another which *appears* to be identical.

THROW To deposit the balance of the cards upon the rest after a shuffle.

TOP CARD The card lying face down on the top of the pack, or the card lying face up on the top of the pack if the pack is presented with all the cards face-up.

TRANSPOSITION The exchange of position between one object and another.

INDEX

ACKNOWLEDGEMENTS

The author would like to thank the following people for their help in the formation of this book: Keren Godfrey for her time, patience and the ultimate transcription of my original manuscript – she had the magic touch; magician and respected historian, Will Ayling, author of many books, grateful thanks for assisting me in The Origins of Magic section; Tim Cox, photographer extraordinaire, responsible for the scores of photographs illustrating this book.